THE PICTURE OF DORIAN GRAY

"What the World Thinks Me"

TWAYNE'S MASTERWORK STUDIES

Robert Lecker, General Editor

THE PICTURE OF DORIAN GRAY

"What the World Thinks Me"

Michael Patrick Gillespie
Marquette University

TWAYNE PUBLISHERS
An Imprint of Simon & Schuster Macmillan
New York

Prentice Hall International
London Mexico City New Delhi Singapore Sydney Toronto

Twayne's Masterwork Studies No. 145

The Picture of Dorian Gray: "What the World Thinks Me"
Michael Patrick Gillespie

Twayne Publishers
An Imprint of Simon & Schuster Macmillan
866 Third Avenue
New York, New York 10022

Library of Congress Cataloging-in-Publication Data

Gillespie, Michael Patrick.
    The picture of Dorian Gray : "what the world thinks of me" / Michael Patrick
Gillespie.
        p.   cm.—(Twayne's masterwork series ; no. 145)
    Includes bibliographical references and index.
    ISBN 0–8057–8375–X (cloth).—ISBN 0–8057–8595–7 (pbk.)
    1. Wilde, Oscar, 1854–1900. Picture of Dirian Gray. 2. Appearance (Philosophy in
literature. I. Title. II. Series: Twayne's masterwork studies ; no. 145.
PR5819.G55   1995
823'.8—dc20   95–7089
                                                                                      CIP

10 9 8 7   (hc)
10 9 8 7 6 5 4 3 2 1 (pb)

Printed in the United States of America

To Ann Gillespie,
who knows the unimportance of being earnest

Contents

Oscar Wilde.

Courtesy of the Irish Tourist Board.

Note on the References and Acknowledgments

All quotations from *The Picture of Dorian Gray* are taken from the 1974 Oxford University Press edition edited by Isobel Murray. Page citations appear in parentheses.

I wish to express my gratitude to John Boly, the Rev. Thaddeus Burch, S.J., John Espy, Paula Gillespie, Donald Lawler, A. Walton Litz, John McCabe, Joan Navarre, David Norris, Kerry Powell, John Rickard, Albert Rivero, and George Sandulescu for generous assistance at various stages of this study. I wish additionally to thank both Robert Lecker and Cindy Buck for their help on opposite ends of this work. I wish also to acknowledge the research support I have received from the William Andrews Clark Memorial Libary, the Princess Grace Irish Library, and the Marquette University Graduate School. Finally, I am deeply grateful to my editor at Twayne, Anne Kiefer, for the energy, enthusiasm, and insight that she brought to this project.

Chronology: Oscar Wilde's Life and Works

1854   Oscar Fingal O'Flahertie Wills Wilde, the second child of the
        well-known Dr. (later Sir) William Robert Wills Wilde and
        Jane Francesca Elgee Wilde, is born in Dublin at 21 Westland
        Row on 16 October. Sir William would gain fame as an
        oculist, aural surgeon, and author of medical texts, travel
        books, and antiquarian studies of Irish folklore and custom.
        Jane Wilde, under her pen name Speranza, contributed patri-
        otic poems to *The Nation* and was well known as a fierce sup-
        porter of Irish independence. Wilde's one older brother,
        William Robert Kingsbury Wills Wilde, born 26 September
        1852, was a remarkably graceful athlete and scholar, and
        Oscar grew up very much in his brother's shadow.

1855   The family moves from Westland Row to a more fashionable
        address, 1 Merrion Square North, where Wilde will spend his
        childhood.

1857   Wilde's younger sister, Isola Francesca Emily Wilde, is born 2
        April, fulfilling Jane Wilde's wish for a daughter. She quickly
        becomes the pet of the family.

1864   Wilde's formal schooling begins in February when he and
        Willie are sent to the newly opened (1859) Portora Royal
        School in Enniskillen, Fermanagh (the school that half a centu-
        ry later would become Samuel Beckett's alma mater). Dr.
        Wilde receives his knighthood.

1867   Isola Wilde develops a fever and dies on 23 February. Wilde is
        deeply affected by her death. All his life he will keep a lock of
        her hair in an elaborately decorated envelope, and one of his
        most moving poems, "Requiescat," captures the lasting sorrow
        that he felt.

1871	Awarded the Portora Gold Medal as the best classical scholar. He leaves Portora Royal School and receives a scholarship to Dublin's Trinity College, where he reads Classics and is tutored by the noted Greek scholar the Rev. J. P. Mahaffy, Junior Fellow, Junior Dean, and Professor of Ancient History.
1874	Wins Trinity's Berkeley Gold Medal for Greek, the college's highest classical award, and earns a scholarship to Magdalen College, Oxford. Enters Magdalen in October and, that fall, joins other students working, at the suggestion of Slade Professor of Fine Art John Ruskin, on constructing a country road in Ferry Hinksey. Wilde is profoundly influenced at Oxford by the aesthetic views of Ruskin and another don, Walter Pater.
1875	Travels in Italy with Mahaffy. During the trip, he writes one of his earliest known poems, "San Miniato."
1876	Wilde's father dies 19 April, and his mother moves to England. Wilde is awarded a first in his Classical Moderations examinations.
1877	Travels to Greece with Mahaffy and returns to England via Rome. In the spring, his first published prose work appears, a *Dublin University Magazine* review of an exhibit at the recently opened Grosvenor Gallery.
1878	His poem "Ravenna" (based on his Italian experiences the previous spring) wins the Newdigate Poetry Prize. When the university has the poem published by Thomas Shrimpton & Son, it becomes Wilde's first published piece of creative work. He receives recognition for having written the year's best examination, thus earning a rare double first on completion of his university work. He leaves Oxford and moves to London.
1879	Briefly returns to Oxford and unsuccessfully attempts to secure election as a fellow at Oxford. In addition, his essay "Historical Criticism in Antiquity" fails to win the Chancellor's Essay Prize. Returns to London in the fall to take up permanent residence.
1880	Embarks on a carefully choreographed campaign to gain a reputation in London society as a wit and a Dandy, and within a short time, caricatures of him begin to appear in *Punch*. He has his first play, *Vera; or the Nihilists*, privately published in London by Ranken.
1881	Privately publishes *Poems*, a collection of his verses that receives generally poor reviews. At the end of November, a

London production of *Vera* is canceled, ostensibly in deference to the feelings of the Russian royal family. Nonetheless, Wilde comes to enjoy a growing reputation as an aesthete. Capitalizing on this notoriety and on satirical characterizations of him in the Gilbert and Sullivan operetta *Patience*, the impresario Richard D'Oyly Carte sends Wilde to America. Wilde departs on 24 December for what will become a widely acclaimed lecture tour.

1882   Arrives in New York on 2 January and spends the year traveling and lecturing to receptive audiences throughout America and Canada. Sails for England on 27 December.

1883   In Paris in February and March completing work on *The Duchess of Padua* (privately printed later in the year), which he writes at the request of the American actress Mary Anderson. After seeing it in final form, she declines to produce it. On 2 August Wilde sails for New York for the 20 August opening of *Vera* at the Union Square Theater. It closes after a one-week run. On 24 September Wilde embarks on an English lecture tour that details his impressions of America. On 25 November he becomes engaged to Constance Lloyd.

1884   Wilde marries Constance Lloyd on 29 May at St. James's Church, Sussex Gardens. The couple honeymoon for a month in Paris.

1885   In January, Wilde and his bride move into 16 Tite Street, Chelsea, a house they will occupy for the next decade. Their first child, Cyril, is born 5 June. Wilde's poem "The Harlot's House" appears in the April issue of the *Dramatic Review*. "Shakespeare and Stage Costume" appears in the May issue of *Nineteenth Century* (reprinted in *Intentions* under the title "The Truth of Masks"). Under pressure to support a growing family, Wilde becomes book review editor of the *Pall Mall Gazette*.

1886   The Wildes' second child, Vyvyan, is born 3 November. Wilde's friendship with Robert Ross begins. Ross will remain a loyal friend for the rest of Wilde's life and will act as literary executor after his death.

1887   Wilde becomes editor (for the next two years) of the magazine *The Woman's World* (after changing its name from *The Lady's World*). Brings a measure of notoriety to the journal by securing contributions from a number of well-known women, including his wife Constance.

1888	A collection of Wilde's stories entitled *The Happy Prince and Other Tales*, some written for his children, appears in May. The volume experiences immediate critical and commercial success.
1889	Publishes the essay "Pen, Pencil and Poison" in January in the *Fortnightly Review*; "The Decay of Lying" in January in *Nineteenth Century*; and "The Portrait of Mr. W. H." in July in *Blackwood's*. Relinquishes his position as editor of *The Woman's World* with the October issue.
1890	The novella version of "The Picture of Dorian Gray" appears in the 20 June issue of *Lippincott's Monthly Magazine*. It is sharply attacked by a number of reviewers, and Wilde spends the next few months writing letters to the editors of various journals defending his work against charges of immorality. "The True Function and Value of Criticism; with Some Remarks on the Value of Doing Nothing: A Dialogue" appears in two parts in the July and September issues of *Nineteenth Century* (reprinted in *Intentions* under the title "The Critic as Artist").
1891	In January the play *The Duchess of Padua* is produced in New York under the title *Guido Ferranti*. The *Fortnightly Review* publishes his essay "The Soul of Man under Socialism" in February and "A Preface to *Dorian Gray*" in March. Wilde's expanded version of *The Picture of Dorian Gray* is published by Ward, Lock in April. He publishes a collection of short stories, *Lord Arthur Savile's Crime and Other Stories*, in July, and another, *A House of Pomegranates*, in November. An Oxford undergraduate magazine, *The Spirit Lamp*, edited by Lord Alfred Douglas, whom Wilde has recently met, publishes the poem "The New Remorse" in December. Wilde also publishes a collection of essays, entitled *Intentions*.
1892	Finishes the French version of *Salomé*, begun in Paris late in 1891. The first of a trio of highly successful social melodramas, *Lady Windermere's Fan*, opens in the West End on 20 February. E. F. S. Pigott, licenser of plays, bans a proposed Sarah Bernhardt production of *Salomé* in London. Although *Punch* makes much ado over Wilde's threat to renounce his citizenship and move to France, the uproar over the banned play subsides rather quickly.
1893	Publishes *Salomé* in its original French. His second social melodrama, *A Woman of No Importance*, opens on 19 April at the Haymarket Theatre, and *Lady Windermere's Fan* is published.

The Spirit Lamp prints two of Wilde's prose sketches, "The House of Judgment" in February and "The Disciple" in June.

1894   His long poem *The Sphinx* is published, as well as an English translation of *Salomé* illustrated by Aubrey Beardsley. *A Woman of No Importance* is published. The *Fortnightly Review* publishes "Poems in Prose" in July, and the *Chameleon*, an Oxford undergraduate magazine that publishes only one issue, prints "Phrases and Philosophies for the Use of the Young" in December.

1895   *The Soul of Man [under Socialism]*, a reprint of the 1891 essay, is privately printed. Wilde's third social melodrama, *The Ideal Husband*, opens 3 January, and the brilliant farce *The Importance of Being Earnest: A Trivial Comedy for Serious People* makes its premier 14 February. On 1 March, at the insistence of Lord Alfred Douglas, Wilde begins an ill-advised libel action against Douglas's father, the ninth Marquess of Queensberry. The trial begins 3 April at the Old Bailey, and on 5 April, after Queensberry's lawyer impugns Wilde's character by establishing his association with a number of young men, Wilde withdraws his suit. That same day he is arrested under a provision of the Criminal Law Amendment Act of 1885 prohibiting "indecent relations" between consenting males. On 24 April creditors force the sale of Wilde's goods at auction. His first trial begins 26 April and ends in a hung jury, but his second trial, beginning 22 May, leads to his conviction on 25 May. He is immediately sentenced to two years at hard labor. Originally imprisoned at Pentonville, Wilde is transferred to H.M. Prison Reading on 20 November.

1896   Wilde's mother dies 3 February, and his wife Constance visits Wilde to bring the news to him. *Salomé* is produced in Paris on 11 February.

1897   Composes *De Profundis*, his long and very bitter letter to Douglas, during his last months in prison. He is released on 19 May and immediately leaves England for France, initially settling in Berneval under the assumed name Sebastian Melmoth. Late in August he meets Douglas in Rouen, and they reconcile. In the fall they spend several months together in Naples.

1898   Wilde's poem *The Ballad of Reading Gaol* is published (initially anonymously) on 13 February. Constance Wilde dies in Genoa on 7 April.

1899   Willie Wilde dies in London in March. *The Importance of Being Earnest* is published in February, and *An Ideal Husband* in July.

1900	On 30 November Wilde dies in Paris at age 46 at the Hotel d'Alsace, of what French doctors diagnosed as encephalitic meningitis. He is buried in Bagneaux Cemetery in Paris. Robert Ross, Reginald Turner, and Lord Alfred Douglas are present at the internment.
1905	An expurgated version of *De Profundis* is published.
1908	*De Profundis [with Additional Matter]* is published. Despite the title, however, portions of the work are suppressed.
1909	At the direction of Robert Ross, Wilde's remains are removed to Père Lachaise Cemetery, Paris, to a tomb designed by Jacob Epstein.
1962	The unexpurgated version of *De Profundis* appears in *The Letters of Oscar Wilde*.

THE
EXTRATEXTUAL MILIEU

1

Historical Context

All art is at once surface and symbol.
Those who go beneath the surface do so at their peril.
Those who read the symbol do so at their peril.
                    Preface to *The Picture of Dorian Gray*

From his birth in Dublin on 16 October 1854 to his death in Paris on 30 November 1900, Oscar Fingal O'Flahertie Wills Wilde lived and wrote in a world bounded and defined by the conventions of the Victorian Age. A full interpretation of his novel *The Picture of Dorian Gray* must begin with an effort to understand the mores of the era that did so much to shape the process of its composition. Of course, the danger of oversimplification accompanies any attempt at an all-encompassing description of the impact of a period spanning nearly seven decades on a single work or author. Nonetheless, careful analysis clearly reveals a number of traits that reflect the influence of important cultural, social, and historical values on Wilde's general artistic standards and specifically on the composition of *The Picture of Dorian Gray*.

Commentators generally agree that the ascendance of the middle class is a defining feature of the Victorian Age, and the virtues and vices of that sector of society dominate perceptions of the era. Middle-class energy, mercantilism, and purpose sparked nearly a century of commercial and colonial expansion that spread English products and values around the globe. The growth of English trade and commerce produced widespread prosperity, which in turn fostered in the middle class a sense of duty and a desire for public esteem. These attitudes informed efforts to forge a stable, well-regulated society, and those efforts in turn enabled England to avoid, for the most part, the political upheavals that periodically shook the governments of Continental Europe during the nineteenth century. The Chartist movement for political reform sputtered to a conclusion in England in 1848 even as midcentury revolutions swept across Europe.

Of course, the parallel pursuits of economic success and public respectability inevitably generated some social tensions. Middle-class prosperity led to a period of materialism that filled Victorian households with goods from around the world and made acquisitiveness a virtue. Further, the self-satisfaction of the age produced an obtuse disregard for social misery that allowed poverty and economic exploitation to flourish, often (though not always) through benign neglect. For instance, the living conditions in the slums of the East End, adjacent to the increasingly prosperous City (London's financial district), were appalling. The lack of concern exhibited by successive British governments led to the formation of private charitable groups like the Salvation Army. Florence Nightingale earned an international reputation through her efforts, both in the Crimea and in England, to overcome profound government apathy toward issues of public health and welfare. Even these efforts, however, had their dark side. George Bernard Shaw's *Major Barbara* (1907), for example, satirizes the complicity of the Salvation Army in maintaining the status quo by keeping the poor from becoming dissatisfied.

Perhaps the most striking evidence of the complex attitudes of the Victorian Age, however, is found in matters of religion and religious practice. Throughout the 1830s and 1840s, prominent theologians of the Oxford Movement like John Henry Newman (who later converted to Roman Catholicism), the clergyman Richard Hurrell Froude, the poet John Keble, and the Oxford don Edward Pusey— attracted a great deal of attention as they strove to define the nature of the Church of England. Though religious issues were central in the Victorian consciousness and the Church played an important part in middle-class life, religious devotion varied widely from individual to individual. According to the census of 1851, for instance, less than 30 percent of the population regularly attended Anglican services, and by 1903 only 19 percent of the London population regularly attended any denominational worship.

With this data before us, identifying Wilde as a Victorian—or anyone else living in that era—raises as many questions as it answers. The very term "Victorian," in fact, is problematic because of the range of responses it elicits. Despite the longevity of Victoria's 64-year reign (1837–1901), the period produced nothing so recognizable as a "spirit of the age." Even those most loyal to the concept of monolithic historical experience find the Victorian era simply too sprawling to consider as a whole.[1] In particular, from the time of the Crimean War (which coincided with Wilde's birth) to the Second Boer War (raging at the time of his death)—conventionally seen as the mid- through the late-Victorian eras—recurring social and political upheavals lend counterpoint to impressions of the stability of the last half of the century and highlight not so much the consistency but the divergence of attitudes among Britons at that time.

Of course, throughout the nineteenth century certain values— duty, respectability, commercial success, middle-class morality—occupied a central position in the Victorian consciousness, but Victorians also became increasingly aware of how frequently the behavior of individuals and of society as a whole undercut the ideals that purportedly characterized their age. Complementing the diverse social views gaining prominence from the mid-Victorian era on, an eclectic intellectual milieu also flourished during Wilde's lifetime and doubtless had a shaping impact on his art. Considering the cultural complexity of the Victorian middle class and the complicated political and social conditions in Ireland, it is no surprise that Oscar Wilde's life and writings reflected attitudes that combine some of the most conventional and contradictory aspects of midcentury society.[2]

For example, at the time of Wilde's birth, his father, Dr. William Wilde, had already become one of the most eminent Irish physicians and antiquarians of the day. Despite Dr. Wilde's strong commitment as a young man to Irish nationalist causes and to Irish efforts to achieve political independence from Great Britain, he was delighted when his medical achievements received formal recognition with his appointment as Surgeon-Oculist to Queen Victoria in 1863 and his selection for knighthood the next year.

The life of Oscar's mother, Jane Francesca Elgee Wilde, also reflected contrasting experiences of the Victorian world. In the 1840s, before marriage and childbearing cut short her literary career, she had gained renown as an ardent advocate of the Irish independence movement by publishing a number of patriotic poems and pamphlets under the pen name Speranza. Like her husband, she was able to reconcile her sentiments as an Irish nationalist with the honors he received from the English crown. For years Lady Wilde remained a prominent figure on the Dublin social scene. At the same time, the family earned a measure of notoriety not only from Lady Wilde's flamboyance but also from scandals relating to Sir William's extramarital affairs, precluding any sort of settled childhood for Oscar, his brother Willie (born in 1852), and his sister Isola (born in 1857).

In short, Wilde was brought up in a world where people were highly original and scrupulously traditional, flamboyant and conventional, rebellious and patriotic. The diffuse elements of Wilde's own temperament manifested themselves early in his life; labeling them idiosyncratic or whimsical is an oversimplification of the complexity of his consciousness. He eventually reconciled these opposites to create the sophisticated, complex persona that would become his own public image in the 1880s and 1890s.[3]

As a student at Trinity College, Dublin, Wilde's early appreciation of paradox grew into a fixture of his character, but in a city filled with eccentrics, his singularity hardly merited attention. Oxford, on the other hand, presented Wilde with a very different world. He entered Magdalen College in October 1874 on an academic grant he had won as a student at Trinity. Although he never openly acknowledged it, his position as a scholarship student, without the status he had enjoyed in Dublin as the brilliant son of a well-known family, set Wilde apart and, initially at least, put him at a disadvantage next to the majority of his upper-middle-class, fee-paying English classmates. If Wilde was bothered, however, he took care not to show it. In fact, he flaunted an individuality that underscored his independence from the cultivated conformity of the behavior of so many around him.

Wilde's life at Oxford nonetheless involved a delicate balancing act that would have a profound impact on his artistic consciousness and especially on the composition of *The Picture of Dorian Gray*. On the one hand, he maintained a pose of whimsical self-absorption, characterized by his observation: "How often I feel how hard it is to live up to my blue china."[4] At the same time, Wilde worked hard to establish his intellectual credentials. He earned a rare double first in successive examinations during his time at the university, but he consciously minimized the effort it took to achieve this honor. In a letter to his friend William Ward, he made his achievement sound almost serendipitous: "The dons are 'astonied' beyond words—the Bad Boy doing so well in the end."[5] Time and again, Wilde managed to be as academically successful as he was self-indulgent, maintaining a duality that committed him exclusively neither to drudgery nor to irresponsibility.

Throughout his adult life, Wilde repeatedly asserted his individuality even as he affirmed his desire to be accepted in society. The public persona he projected encompassed a range of often contradictory attitudes: sensitive critic, flamboyant connoisseur, careless artist, devoted family man, self-centered hedonist. At the same time, these poses quite accurately reflected Victorian modes of behavior. Wilde was distinguishing himself as one intimately aware of the subtlest nuances of English society yet sufficiently distant from it to issue dispassionate if hardly disinterested commentary. This chameleonlike response to various societal situations came out of a lifelong habit of balancing accommodation and individuality.

Tutors like John Ruskin and Walter Pater provided Wilde with the scholarly structure for his burgeoning aesthetic views, but as countless anecdotes confirm, Wilde established himself as a commanding intellectual and social figure at the university almost from the day he arrived.[6] Later, Wilde would refer to his time at Oxford as the happiest period of his life, and he would memorialize his undergraduate days in works like "Magdalen Walks," a poem subsequently praised by Pater.

When Wilde went to London in 1878, he found its aesthetic milieu much more complex and competitive than the academic atmosphere of Oxford. Nonetheless, gaining a measure of recognition—especially for an individual with Wilde's wit and self-confidence—proved easier than might have been expected. In fact, as some contemporaries would sardonically note, Wilde acquired an artistic reputation well before he produced any work of genuine merit.

Wilde's initial success says as much about the changing creative atmosphere of England in the 1880s as it does about his individual talent. As John Gross has noted about Victorian society at this time: "Whatever one puts it down to—economic difficulties, foreign competition—it is undoubtedly possible to detect by the 1880's a widespread faltering of Victorian self-confidence, a new edginess and uncertainty about the future. Among writers, such a climate might have been supposed to favor a mood of determined realism, and so, in some cases, it did. But the commonest reaction was withdrawal, a retreat into nostalgia, exoticism, fine writing, *belles-lettres*."[7] In a society characterized by transformation in economic conditions and a popular attitude toward art that alternated between belligerent defense of conventional aesthetic values and timid insecurity in the face of imaginative innovation, Wilde quickly established himself as an independent voice and, in time, a formidable literary figure. He publicly proclaimed his genius, privately printed a volume of his own poems, effusively lauded the charms of Lillie Langtry, and artfully demonstrated his wit as a guest at dinner parties.

Once he had presented himself to London as the spokesman of new aesthetic standards, the role quickly took on a life of its own. Parodies of Wilde and his artistic opinions appeared in *Punch* and in the Gilbert and Sullivan production *Patience*. Rather than undermining his renown, these jibes validated and enhanced his achievement. In fact, such spoofs underscored his similarity to a longstanding figure in Victorian society, the Dandy.

In assuming this role, Wilde drew upon the features of the archetypal dandies who had emerged over the course of the nineteenth century—the mindless clotheshorses of the Brummell era, the incisively witty Count d'Orsay, and the degraded caricatures that appear in

Dickens. He refined these traits into a character who artfully reflected the society from which he had emerged, a figure who would amuse and titillate his fellow Victorians, even stretch their social tolerance, but would never, they felt (at least until they were confronted with the disclosures of Wilde's 1895 trials), go beyond the limits imposed by society.

In short, Wilde became famous as a figure whose nature combined conventional and unconventional views, anticipating the more radical characterizations of the same type that would appear in *The Picture of Dorian Gray*. In contrast to the characters Dorian Gray and Lord Henry Wotton, however, Wilde never hesitated to question orthodox thinking and behavior. At the same time, he never seriously challenged the social primacy of orthodoxy.

Wilde's paradoxical nature determined the sort of book *The Picture of Dorian Gray* would become, for it predisposed him to explore the complexities and inconsistencies of his age. Further, Wilde's renown as a critic of conventional attitudes created certain expectations with the Victorian public. Any attempt to write from a perspective markedly different from the one he daily assumed in society would surely have met with rejection. Wilde summed up his view of the complex relationship between art and life in remarks made to André Gide: "I have put my genius into my life; I've only put my talent into my works."[8]

Whether his work reflected talent or genius remains open to debate. Nonetheless, by the late 1880s Wilde had established his artistic reputation through a series of essays, aimed predominantly at a middle-class audience, that observed and critiqued the studied inconsistencies of upper-class life. By the time the novella "The Picture of Dorian Gray" appeared in *Lippincott's* in 1890—followed the next year by what is now the more familiar novel-length version—Wilde had fully prepared Victorian society for his complexity and exuberance. Although initial critical response varied widely, Wilde's novel undeniably achieved popular and artistic success by evoking the aesthetic equivalent of the Dandy's nature. Every chapter of the book makes a series of baroque images and experiences both accessible and acceptable by grounding them in the familiar territory of conventional life.

Wilde's originality, however, went beyond replication in his art of the eccentric persona of the Dandy he assumed in public. His intellect, like his writing, depended for its successful expression on conveying multiple points of view. In seeking the creative stimulus of a range of experiences, Wilde, with calculated assurance, moved easily through a range of social strata, collecting a variety of perspectives on Victorian life. While cultivating an aristocratic mien in his public life and in his writing, he acknowledged his middle-class sensibilities, even as he indulged a fascination for entertaining young men from the lower classes, a practice Wilde labeled "feasting with panthers" (*LOW*, 492).

By gaining so much prominence and admiration with a minimum of creative effort, however, Wilde became for some a perpetual target of resentment. The painter James A. McNeill Whistler probably spoke for many Londoners when in frustration he questioned Wilde's credentials as an artist. "What has Oscar in common with Art? except that he dines at our tables and picks from our platters the plums for the pudding he peddles in the provinces. Oscar—the amiable, irresponsible, esurient Oscar—with no more sense of a picture than of the fit of a coat, has the courage of the opinions—of others!"[9] Although Whistler's characterization contained a measure of truth, in the end it proved an inadequate assessment of Wilde's artistic persona. It missed the point that Wilde's work served as an extension of his nature and grew out of the Victorian world that defined that nature. At the same time, Wilde's life appears in *The Picture of Dorian Gray* obliquely, providing no easy correlations between autobiographical and fictional material.

Much has been made, for example, of the impact on Wilde's writing of his attraction to the conflicting aesthetics of his two prominent Oxford tutors, John Ruskin and Walter Pater. The views of these two men are far too complex to summarize, but they can be distinguished here by their attitudes toward the aims of art. Ruskin saw art from the perspective of an idealist: art is good when it inspires people to be better. Pater, on the other hand, took the position of a materialist: art is good when it gives us pleasure.[10] In tracing Wilde's intellectual and artistic development, however, it is not useful to pit Ruskin's impact against Pater's. Wilde himself seemed inclined to modify and incorporate the views of both men into his artistic consciousness. He noted his inclination toward pluralism in a letter to Ralph Payne: "I am so glad you like that strange coloured book of mine: it contains much of me in it. Basil Hallward is what I think I am: Lord Henry what the world thinks me: Dorian what I would like to be—in other ages perhaps" (LOW, 352).

It is precisely this sort of ambiguity that makes *The Picture of Dorian Gray* such an interesting reflection of the world from which it emerged. In fact, as events in Wilde's own life would conclusively demonstrate, his society could tolerate such ambiguity far more easily than it could handle some certitudes. As I demonstrate in later chapters of this study, the appeals to multiple points of view that permeate the narrative of *The Picture of Dorian Gray* allow for interpretations that broaden the range of aesthetic pleasures to be derived from the novel.

By the same token, the novel allowed its immediate audience, the Victorian public, to observe Wilde's fascinating lifestyle—which was surrounded with an air of uncertainty—with no need to acknowledge any affront to contemporary morality. When in the spring of 1895 Wilde's unsuccessful libel suit against the Marquess of Queensberry, father of Lord Alfred Douglas, led to Wilde's own trial and imprisonment for "immoral acts," any ambiguity in his public pose vanished in the harsh illumination of the judicial proceedings. His audience had so linked his social persona with their experience of reading his works that the clarification of his sexual disposition undermined the effect of his canon.

Wilde's conviction immediately changed the public's response to his writing. Two plays in the midst of highly successful runs in West End theaters—*An Ideal Husband* and *The Importance of Being Earnest*—were closed almost at once, and his published works disappeared from bookstores, seemingly overnight. Upon his release, after serving two years in prison, Wilde immediately went to the Continent. Over the next three years, he spent most of his time in France, assuming the role of literary exile. During that time, he wrote only "The Ballad of Reading Gaol," a poem based on his prison experiences. *De Profundis*, his long and bitter letter to Lord Alfred Douglas composed during his final months in Reading, would not appear until after his death. Despite his prolific output, by the time he died his reputation had been blasted.

Only as the years have put distance between judgments on Wilde's life and interpretations of his work has that writing been revaluated. As I discuss in chapter 2, later readers have shown an attentiveness to a variety of features in Wilde's oeuvre: representations of conventional archetypal concerns, reflections of serious moral imperfection, and articulations of visionary social concern.

2

The Importance of the Work in Defining the Context of Ambiguity

The nineteenth century dislike of Realism is the rage of Caliban seeing his own face in a glass.

The nineteenth century dislike of Romanticism is the rage of Caliban not seeing his own face in a glass.

Preface to *The Picture of Dorian Gray*

In its fundamental structure, *The Picture of Dorian Gray* stands apart from other nineteenth-century works of fiction. Through the multiple perspectives imbedded in its narrative, it encourages diverse readings, anticipating the direction taken by the experimental efforts of twentieth-century fiction.[1] Instead of presenting a prescriptive cause-and-effect discourse that emphasizes one invariable interpretation, Wilde's novel involves the reader's imagination in the creation of meaning. Comparing *The Picture of Dorian Gray* with a more conventional novel—a murder mystery, for example—reveals this process at work.

In a murder mystery, the narrative moves forward in a calculated, linear fashion. Although a clever reader can anticipate the solution of the mystery by deciphering the clues the author planted in the narrative, the reader can never expand the scope of the narrative beyond what is presented on the printed page. The mystery novel simply does not support any response that changes the story the author plotted.

Wilde's novel, on the other hand, takes a far different approach. Rather than following the narrative model of presenting a clear, unambiguous account of events, it substitutes a structure in which multiple meanings are possible in every reading of the novel. *The Picture of Dorian Gray* changes the traditionally passive reader into an actively involved figure, allowing him or her to decide how to incorporate independent ideas in the narrative into an interpretation that permits different, sometimes even contradictory perspectives to coexist. As a result, Wilde's novel rejects the idea that fiction can be read by progressively narrowing the interpretive options until only a single meaning remains.

This tendency toward diverse responses asserts itself in *The Picture of Dorian Gray* even before the narrative begins. The preface offers the reader a page and a half of aphoristic phrases arranged in no apparent order and only loosely connected to one another.[2] While Wilde makes no attempt to present the preface as a guide for reading his novel, its very makeup challenges conventional assumptions about reading and cannot fail to influence the reader's impressions of the rest of *The Picture of Dorian Gray*. (Examples of the material included in the preface appear as epigraphs for the first three chapters of this book, and in the final chapter I offer a detailed examination of the preface's impact on our understanding of the novel.)

Immediately following the preface, the novel opens in a traditional narrative exposition format and in a style of descriptive extravagance that will punctuate the remainder of the novel: "The studio was filled with the rich odour of roses, and when the light summer wind stirred amidst the trees of the garden there came through the open door the heavy scent of the lilac, or the more delicate perfume of the pink-flowering thorn" (1). The single sentence that takes up this entire paragraph with unchecked exuberance signals an intention both to develop the story through conventional techniques and to disrupt that development through extravagant elaborations.

As *The Picture of Dorian Gray* progresses, its narrative continues to alternate between an orthodox fictional structure and experimental stylistic digressions—seen perhaps most clearly in the extended sensual descriptions in chapter 11—balancing a pure love of language against the need to forward the plot. Even in apparently set pieces, like the preternatural representation of Dorian's picture, a dual function emerges. As the portrait changes its form over the course of the novel, it introduces a fantastic element into the plot, drawing upon the familiar Gothic forms that writers like Wilkie Collins used so effectively and that operate as subtext in so many of Dickens's works.

In fact, over the course of the novel a series of distinctive styles appear that both reinforce conventional expectations and raise possibilities for a range of new interpretive responses. This aspect of the novel's composition made a great impression on the Irish writer James Joyce, who, in a 19 August 1906 letter to his brother Stanislaus, summed up his feelings with an analogy every bit as exuberant as Wilde's own prose: "Some chapters are like Huysmans, catalogued atrocities, lists of perfumes and instruments. The central idea is fantastic."[3]

The thematic structure of *The Picture of Dorian Gray* also presents the reader with interpretive challenges. On the one hand, the narrative develops standard topics familiar to the majority of readers. Perhaps the most basic is the classic struggle between good and evil, particularly characteristic of popular Victorian works. One sees this conflict dramatized time and again throughout the narrative, and no more forcefully than when Lord Henry Wotton tempts Dorian with a radically different vision of the world in the archetypal Edenic setting of Basil Hallward's garden. Other compositional features also seem to represent attitudes common to Victorian writing. Although, for example, much of the novel's action concentrates exclusively on the upper classes, almost every character is aware of the starkly delineated differences between social groups. One sees this consciousness in the obvious distinctions made between Dorian and the Vane family; in Dorian's feeling of perverse pleasure at debauching himself among the lower classes; and, in chapter 6, in Sibyl and James Vane's discomfort over walking in Hyde Park at a time when members of the upper classes promenade there.

Despite the familiar nature of these subjects, Wilde does not treat traditional topics in a predictable manner, as illustrated, for example, in his characterizations of the work's central character. In the opening chapter, Basil Hallward gives a glowing account of Dorian's success as a model. Although the young man effortlessly assumes a range of roles while posing for Basil's paintings, he always retains the enigmatic aura that distinguishes him from all that he imitates. As the narrative progresses, Dorian continues to play roles, emerging as an independent character who disregards the strictures laid down by established social institutions. His essential nature, however, remains a mystery for the reader to unravel. Dorian tells Basil as much when he explains why the death of Sybil Vane has not made him inconsolable: "To become the spectator of one's own life, as Harry says, is to escape the suffering of life. . . . I am what I am. There is nothing more to be said" (110). Readers must decide how to delineate "I am what I am" in order to come to an assessment of Dorian.

Other characters place similar interpretive responsibilities on the reader by displaying the same sort of behavior: Lord Henry, for example, may seem far more lethargic than Dorian and more given to speculation than to action. Nonetheless, his physical indolence has no effect on the multiple points of view that distinguish his nature. As Basil says early in the novel, "You are an extraordinary fellow. You never say a moral thing, and you never do a wrong thing" (4). Although in his naïveté Basil goes a bit far in overlooking Lord Henry's flaws, he accurately points out the diverse representations of self that his friend offers to the world around him. Further, Basil's own regard for the power of individual judgment shows readers that assumptions about the Victorian concern for public opinion and esteem no longer serve as the only suitable guidelines for assessing character in *The Picture of Dorian Gray*.

All in all, the reader finds throughout the novel a consistent emphasis on its ability to support a number of equally plausible readings. Chapter 2, for example, presents several different characters as perhaps the one responsible for initiating the pattern of behavior Dorian will follow throughout *The Picture of Dorian Gray*. Basil's fawning devotion to Dorian's beauty supports the idea that such unrestrained flattery, no matter how innocent Basil's intentions may be, undermines the young man's judgment. On the other hand, Lord Henry's sociopathic curiosity about Dorian's nature offers the equally plausible possibility that Dorian finds himself overwhelmed by an amoral intellect whose reasoning proves too subtle and sophisticated to resist. Still another possible interpretation originates in Dorian's own behavior: in his arrogantly naive pride, perhaps he bears full responsibility for his own downfall. The implications of each of these points of view will be explored in the second half of this study. For now, it is important to note only that each perspective derives its validity from the system of values the reader uses as the basis for deriving meaning.

With no way to rank one interpretation over another—other than by making a subjective and ultimately arbitrary choice—all three remain equally viable readings; one cannot dismiss any of them. Even when a reader makes the calculated choice to see *The Picture of Dorian Gray* in a particular way—with Lord Henry as the novel's chief villain, for instance—he or she cannot avoid retaining, in some form of suspended awareness, a perception of the other, equally valid meanings that can be derived from the narrative.

This challenge to the routine application of conventional values is most strikingly illustrated in the novel's alternative ethical system, "New Hedonism," which makes pluralism an almost inevitable response. Lord Henry Wotton articulates this concept early in the narrative: "Live! Live the wonderful life that is in you! Let nothing be lost upon you. Be always searching for new sensations. Be afraid of nothing. . . . [Wilde's ellipses] A new Hedonism—that is what our century wants. You might be its visible symbol. With your personality there is nothing you could not do. The world belongs to you for a season" (22). New Hedonism, an elaboration on the ideas of one of Wilde's Oxford tutors, Walter Pater, expresses a full commitment to aesthetic pleasure with no concern for the consequences: "To burn always with this hard, gemlike flame, to maintain this ecstasy, is success in life."[4] New Hedonism rests on the assumption that any action is justifiable, for "experience is everything," and it introduces into the narrative an ethical system radically different from conventional expectations.

> Yes: there was to be, as Lord Henry had prophesied, a new
> Hedonism that was to recreate life, and to save it from that harsh,
> uncomely puritanism that is having, in our own day, its curious
> revival. It was to have its service of the intellect, certainly; yet, it
> was never to accept any theory or system that would involve the
> sacrifice of any mode of passionate experience. Its aim, indeed, was
> to be experience itself, and not the fruits of experience, sweet or
> bitter as they might be. Of the asceticism that deadens the senses,
> as of the vulgar profligacy that dulls them, it was to know nothing.
> But it was to teach man to concentrate himself upon the moments
> of a life that is itself but a moment. (130)

In this way, New Hedonism competes with conventional morality for the right to designate the perspective best suited to interpret the behavior of the characters in the novel.

Paradoxically, even as some elements in *The Picture of Dorian Gray* put forward an alternative to common societal values, others call unconventional attitudes into question. Pangs of guilt cause Dorian to swing between remorse and exultation throughout most of the novel, and an uncharacteristic moral torpor seems to engulf Lord Henry in the work's final chapters. At the same time, the narrative maintains its insistent criticism of Victorian society, making it impossible to explain any wavering in Lord Henry or Dorian as reversion to the traditional values they have opposed throughout.

The uniqueness of *The Picture of Dorian Gray* lies in part in the ambivalent feelings created by the clash of New Hedonism and conventional morality, feelings that reach their peak near the end of the novel, in chapter 19, when both Dorian and Lord Henry express broad dissatisfaction with the practicality of codes in general. Each man seems uncomfortable with the idea that a single ethical system—however defined—can prescribe satisfying modes of behavior, and each expresses uncertainty over the individual's relation with the world.

With the assumptions that govern both society and the central figures of the novel called into question, yet another perspective for reading the novel emerges. The reader cannot overlook the aura of pessimism when even the death of Dorian in the final lines of the narrative seems to parody rather than affirm literary and moral conventions. The artificial, deus ex machina effect suggests that no single point of view can fully understand the world of *The Picture of Dorian Gray*.

This last, highly pessimistic perspective in *The Picture of Dorian Gray*—a hopelessness about the ability of any individual to follow a personal moral system—comes very close to evoking the nihilism of some more contemporary thinkers. (French existential writers like Camus and Sartre come immediately to mind, as well as the Irish author Samuel Beckett and the Americans John Irving and Thomas Pynchon.) While Dorian, Lord Henry, and even Basil Hallward use an urbane self-confidence to assert themselves throughout much of the narrative, nihilistic tendencies intrude, first obliquely and then with increasing directness, over the latter half of the work. From the murder of Basil Hallward onward, Dorian finds no satisfaction in living the life prescribed by his society. Nevertheless, as he clearly reveals in his conversations with Basil, Alan Campbell, and James Vane, he cannot escape a measure of guilt when he ignores its strictures.

Recognition of these diverse points of view in the narrative of *The Picture of Dorian Gray*, however, does not lead to an easy decision as to which perspective should dominate readings of the novel. The reader cannot sustain the assumptions underlying any one perspective over those of any other. Rather than marring the interpretive potential of the work, however, this resistance to closure is what gives the novel its singular importance. The complex narrative structure of formal and thematic elements truly sets *The Picture of Dorian Gray* apart. Wilde's discourse does not simply displace conventional interpretive perspectives with iconoclastic ones. It acknowledges both the impact of a variety of views and the ability of individual readers to maintain simultaneously a sense of multiple responses to the novel.

The Picture of Dorian Gray, a work of literary consequence beyond its specific and immediate aesthetic impact, exemplifies an important shift in critical thinking. By offering a range of options to readers sensitive to the tradition of modern literature, Wilde's novel overturns the idea that we must work to establish a single, dominant meaning. Instead, it allows us to recognize and celebrate the interpretive alternatives, whose variety enhances rather than mars aesthetic pleasure.

The Picture of Dorian Gray continues to profoundly influence modern writers and to retain the interest of contemporary readers precisely because it leaves itself open to a variety of views, a condition of so much of the world around us. While we can, of course, give preference to one interpretation of the novel over another, we can never fully exclude from our consciousness the effect of alternative readings. Nor, as the novel repeatedly demonstrates, should we wish to.

3

The Critical Reception

The critic is he who can translate into another manner or a new material his impression of beautiful things.

The highest as the lowest form of criticism is a mode of autobiography.

Those who find ugly meanings in beautiful things are corrupt without being charming. This is a fault.

Those who find beautiful meanings in beautiful things are the cultivated. For these there is hope.

They are the elect to whom beautiful things mean only Beauty.
                                        Preface to *The Picture of Dorian Gray*

Wilde wrote the novella "The Picture of Dorian Gray" at the request of one of the editors of Philadelphia's *Lippincott's Monthly Magazine*, J. Marshall Stoddart, and the magazine's American readers so enjoyed it that the print run of the July 1890 issue, in which it appeared, quickly sold out. It was simultaneously published by Ward, Lock and

Company in England, where it received a far different response. Within a few days of publication, several reviewers subjected "The Picture of Dorian Gray" to intense censure. These initial assessments, though often based in the constricted scrupulousness of the individual critic, unquestionably set a pattern for many of the responses that would follow.

One of the first of these reviews, published in the *St. James's Gazette*, clearly illustrates how a sense of personal moral outrage can become the basis for a general aesthetic condemnation. The opening paragraph of this article, entitled "A Study in Puppydom," establishes the anonymous critic's views with a sweeping denouncement that pronounces the work unfit for general consumption:

> Time was (it was in the '70's) when we talked about Mr. Oscar Wilde; time came (it was in the '80's) when he tried to write poetry and, more adventurous, we tried to read it; time is when we had forgotten him, or only remember him as the late editor of the *Woman's World*—a part for which he was singularly unfitted, if we are to judge him by the work which he has been allowed to publish in *Lippincott's Magazine* and which Messrs. Ward, Lock, & Co. have not been ashamed to circulate in Great Britain. Not being curious in ordure, and not wishing to offend the nostrils of decent persons, we do not propose to analyse "The Picture of Dorian Gray": that would be to advertise the developments of an esoteric prurience. Whether the Treasury of the Vigilance Society will think it worth while to prosecute Mr. Oscar Wilde or Messrs. Ward, Lock & Co., we do not know; but on the whole we hope they will.[1]

Another piece, characterized by the same tone of condescending nastiness, appeared a short time later in the *Daily Chronicle*. Also unsigned, it echoed the review in the *St. James's Gazette* in its overconfident impulse to categorize Wilde's work with a barrage of insults camouflaged as high-minded indignation (although even in his self-righteousness, the *Daily Chronicle*'s critic could not help acknowledging the worth he saw in the story): "Dulness and dirt are the chief features of

Lippincott's this month. The element in it that is unclean, though undeniably amusing, is furnished by Mr. Oscar Wilde's story of *The Picture of Dorian Gray*. It is a tale spawned from the leprous literature of the French *Decadents*—a poisonous book, the atmosphere of which is heavy with the mephitic odours of moral and spiritual putrefaction" (*Critical Heritage*, 72). Other popular journals, like the *Scots Observer* and *Punch*, quickly followed suit and produced reviews with the same aura of heavy-handed moral disapproval (*Critical Heritage*, 74–77).

Wilde and his publishers took these judgments quite seriously and moved quickly to answer them: Wilde wrote letters of rebuttal, and more flattering reviews were undertaken by sympathetic readers.[2] In addition, while preparing the expanded version for publication in 1891, Wilde acted to forestall a renewal of the previous attacks by writing and separately publishing the preface to *The Picture of Dorian Gray* one month before the book's publication and a few months after the initial controversy erupted. In the preface, Wilde very subtly transforms a number of the issues raised by those who had sharply criticized the novella, redefining them in a fashion more favorable to his own approach. However, the complex interpretation outlined in the preface was not easily reconciled with most readings of the novel, and in consequence Wilde's framing of the issues has remained on the periphery of efforts to derive meaning from the work.

Despite the obvious appearance of a conflict of interest, *Lippincott's* unabashedly printed two reviews in the September 1890 issue—by Anne H. Wharton and by Julian Hawthorne—that lauded *The Picture of Dorian Gray* by mixing substantial praise and thoughtful assessments of Wilde's story. Nonetheless, an unmistakably defensive tone characterized these essays as well as the famous review of the expanded version of *The Picture of Dorian Gray* that Walter Pater wrote for the November 1891 issue of *The Bookman*—despite the fact that he not only was Wilde's former tutor but had advised him during the process of revising *The Picture of Dorian Gray*.[3] Unfortunately, these tactics failed to dispel the impression left by the initial attacks. Additionally, as a number of critics have noted, these early assessments most certainly exerted a direct impact on Wilde's revisions as he expanded "The Picture of Dorian Gray" into a full-length novel.[4]

Most significantly, however, the fierce debate over the novel's moral postures so thoroughly shaped reader expectations that the issues first raised in 1890 continued for decades to exert a strong influence on the work's critical reception.[5] In consequence, early readers approached *The Picture of Dorian Gray* making two assumptions: that the novel's narrative presented a series of choices that the reader had to make to form an interpretation, and that this process of selecting specific options progressively narrowed and refined the reader's interpretation. The durability of such assumptions is reflected in their persistence throughout the first 75 years of criticism of the novel. Only in the last quarter-century, in a more diverse intellectual atmosphere, have contemporary interpretations broken from the assumption that a single dominant reading can provide a full explanation of the novel.[6]

The earliest scholarly writings about Wilde and his work generally relied on rudimentary biographical analyses that drew heavily on the often salacious—and always self-serving—recollections of his former friends and acquaintances. The reminiscences of two writers in particular, Frank Harris and Lord Alfred Douglas, offer the most glaring examples of this sort of excessive and inaccurate critique.[7] Among the memorialists, Robert Sherard stands as a notable exception to the trend of slandering Wilde; in a series of biographical and autobiographical books written between 1902 and 1934, he did his utmost to defend his friend's character against all charges of moral impropriety.[8] For all his noble intentions, however, Sherard's recollections are no more dependable or accurate than those of any of the men determined to undermine Wilde's character.

Whatever their attitude, these rememberers of things past in fact paid relatively little direct attention to *The Picture of Dorian Gray*, or to any of Wilde's writings for that matter. Instead, they generally concentrated on a self-congratulatory reconstruction of the events of Wilde's life. The popularity—or notoriety—of these recollections established two significant points in the critical consciousness of many readers: the assumption that the biographical details of Wilde's life were closely connected to the events in his fiction, and the assumption that any interpretation of Wilde's works involved either accepting or condemning his personal behavior. (With all this emphasis on biographical detail, Arthur Ransome's 1912 book, *Oscar Wilde: A Critical Study*, praised by Ian Fletcher and John Stokes as the first legitimate interpretive examination of Wilde's canon, stands as a notable and rare exception to the trend in the earliest Wilde criticism to feature memoirs over scholarship.)[9]

Whatever interpretive drawbacks have arisen from these biographical studies, however, over the years they have unquestionably stimulated a great deal of interest in Wilde's novel. More specifically, the writings of early memorialists—Harris, Douglas, Gide, Sherard, and others—established a pool of literary recollections from which subsequent, critically sophisticated analyses have drawn to enhance their own explications. The most recent—and by any standard one of the most objective—is Richard Ellmann's interpretive study of Wilde's life and works, which superbly illustrates how a scholar can draw on the early biographies and memoirs without succumbing to their reductivism.[10] From the general observations of Richard Ellmann to the more focused views of Robert Boyle, efforts to use the biographical details of Wilde's life to inform interpretations of his novel have continued over the years, and substantial and illuminating biographical work continues to appear.[11]

When the last of the men and women who had known Wilde became too old to continue to record their recollections, a number of discerning, culturally based examinations of *The Picture of Dorian Gray* started to emerge. One of the first of these studies was Frances Winwar's *Oscar Wilde and the Yellow Nineties* (1940), which appeared in England just 40 years after Wilde's death.[12] This study of the fin-de-siècle literary scene reexamined the social conditions that shaped Wilde's canon and set the pattern for the numerous cultural studies of Wilde's work that would appear over the next half-century.

In the late 1950s and early 1960s, a new generation of scholars, following Winwar's example, offered interesting hybrids of the earlier approaches. Pictorial biographies, for example, used a striking combination of elements—illustrations evoking the late-Victorian age, abbreviated accounts of Wilde's life, and thumbnail sketches of his major works—to present an eclectic overview of his artistic achievement.

They began to suggest strategies for coming to grips with the multiple perspectives of his canon.[13]

Over the next two decades, scholars began to exploit the potential of cultural studies by refining conceptions of the relation of Wilde's novel to the world from which it emerged, such as in J. E. Chamberlin's *Ripe Was the Drowsy Hour* (1977). This mode of inquiry reached its peak with Regenia Gagnier's detailed examination of the world from which Wilde's canon emerged, *Idylls of the Marketplace: Oscar Wilde and the Victorian Public* (1986), a work that outstandingly illustrates the interpretive benefits of such efforts.[14]

A more direct application of the ideas of cultural context appeared in a series of interpretations of *The Picture of Dorian Gray* that pursued meaning through overtly moral examination of Wilde's canon. Studies like Christopher Nassaar's *Into the Demon Universe* (1974) and Philip Cohen's *The Moral Vision of Oscar Wilde* (1978) shun the superficial application of conventional social attitudes and instead offer readings directly informed by traditional Judeo-Christian values.[15] Such views may seem unduly narrow and overly moralistic to some contemporary readers. Nonetheless, they present fully formed and systematic interpretations of the cultural context that give equal focus to Wilde's work and to his life.

At about the same time that early sociological and cultural studies were beginning to suggest responses to *The Picture of Dorian Gray* that went beyond simple analogies between aspects of the novel and biographical facts, Epifanio San Juan, Jr., published the first book-length examination of Wilde's canon that concentrated on the texts themselves. San Juan employed conventional methods of close reading to support his interpretations of *The Picture of Dorian Gray*. His work deserves recognition for a number of reasons, not the least being its sophisticated response to Wilde's writing. Perhaps most significantly, however, San Juan's study showed that, without resorting to a range of biographical, cultural, psychological, or spiritual considerations, New Critics could derive meaning from Wilde's novel simply through careful intratextual analysis.[16]

As Wilde's canon rather than his life increasingly became the topic of literary concern, other approaches to *The Picture of Dorian*

Gray began to appear. A number of critics followed traditional archetypal methods and compared the work's characters with previous literary and mythological figures; Faust was the most popular but by no means the only model considered.[17] Like the New Critical readings of the novel, the archetypal approach provided more evidence that *The Picture of Dorian Gray* could sustain sophisticated critical examination.

From the 1980s onward, a number of highly inventive critics have applied a range of methods to Wilde's novel. Some of the most innovative approaches clearly reflect the influence of radical postmodern thinkers like Michel Foucault, whose views have guided a number of informative extratextual studies based on sexual orientation. More specifically, Eve Kosofsky Sedgwick's pioneering study about male relations in Victorian society, *Between Men* (1986), laid the intellectual groundwork for sharply focused examinations of homosexual perspectives in Wilde's novel. Within a year of the appearance of Sedgwick's book, both Ed Cohen and Richard Dellamora published important essays focusing on aspects of sexual orientation as keys to reading *The Picture of Dorian Gray*.[18] Other critics followed with analyses of the homosexual features of a range of Wilde's works, introducing illuminating perspectives that had been previously ignored.

More than just sexual orientation informed the sociological criticism of *The Picture of Dorian Gray* that appeared throughout the 1980s. Camille Paglia, for example, while taking note of sexual issues, used them as a basis for exploring the rhetorical implications of Wilde's narrative. For Regenia Gagnier, on the other hand, cultural studies meant developing responses not only along sexual but also along materialist and ideological lines.[19]

Ian Small has clearly identified a range of approaches to the cultural context from which *The Picture of Dorian Gray* emerged. Despite their breadth and variety, the insights each approach offers are still inherently narrow and restrictive. Of course, as amply demonstrated in the more traditional approaches offered by Kerry Powell, cultural criticism does not necessarily lead to unconventional readings. As Powell's careful scholarship demonstrates, the insights provided by cultural criticism more often than not provoke further study rather than present interpretive resolution.[20]

Finally, perhaps the most fundamentally important aspect of Wilde criticism has received the least attention. Detailed scholarly examinations of Wilde's manuscripts first began when the New York Public Library published a two-volume edition of *The Importance of Being Earnest* that contained the early version of the play ("Lady Lancing") in typescript and manuscript facsimiles as well as the intermediate four-act version.[21] More recently, textual critics have turned their attention to *The Picture of Dorian Gray* through the efforts of insightful scholars like Isobel Murray and Donald L. Lawler; in addition, John Espy's work analyzing the Wilde holdings at the William Andrews Clark Memorial Library laid the foundation for a growing interest in genetic studies.[22]

Currently, the challenge to contemporary readers of *The Picture of Dorian Gray* is not so much to find different ways of interpreting the novel—however useful a goal that may be—as to cultivate multiple perspectives. Rather than generate yet another view of *The Picture of Dorian Gray* (the sausage-making approach to criticism), contemporary readers need to combine the range of possibilities already identified into coherent responses. In the second part of this study, I suggest strategies for implementing just such an approach.

READINGS
AND REREADINGS

A Prefatory Note

In the following four chapters, which draw upon concepts for reading alluded to in the book's first part, I seek to expand on those concepts to produce a series of related approaches to understanding *The Picture of Dorian Gray*. While these chapters share common assumptions and offer responses to Wilde's novel that are often complementary, they also function independently. In the first part of this study, I have emphasized the idea that Wilde's narrative actively encourages the reader to view the work from a range of perspectives, in turn fostering multiple interpretations. The following readings present three of the many different approaches a reader might take to *The Picture of Dorian Gray*. In the concluding chapter, I offer a close reading of the preface in an attempt to suggest ways of reconciling the diverse responses the narrative elicits.

Chapter 4, "The Imaginative Response Invited by *The Picture of Dorian Gray*," questions the assumption that one reads to find the meaning hidden beneath the surface of Wilde's narrative. Specifically, in looking at how a reader's background and expectations shape one's response to the novel, this chapter examines how strong, sometimes conflicting interpretive possibilities emerge from the differing points of view the discourse seems to encourage. These different perspectives become particularly evident when the reader considers the interpretive consequences of the range of opinions on Dorian's nature held by various characters. Traditional evaluative standards still apply—this character is the hero, that one is the villain—but their application can produce sharply different results, depending on one's point of view.

Chapter 5, "Ethics and Aesthetics," looks at material that exists outside the novel but nonetheless influences our readings. It draws attention to the impact of social, cultural, and historical conditions on the responses of both the author and the reader by focusing on a central feature of the narrative: New Hedonism. When the tradition of Western morality operating in both the mind of the reader and that of the author confronts an innovative ethical system—New Hedonism—the reader's expectations can play off the author's to produce the opportunity for diverse interpretations.

Of course, while chapters 4 and 5 point up the pluralism the reader encounters in the novel, the internal and external elements that shape reader response to *The Picture of Dorian Gray* do more than simply encourage diverse interpretations. These features draw attention to the operation of the narrative of *The Picture of Dorian Gray* on several distinct but equally valid interpretive levels—leading us in turn to consider how these elements interact to contribute to any particular view of the discourse.

Chapter 6, "The Resonance of Sensuality," elaborates on the influence of such a distinctively diverse narrative structure. Specifically, it looks at how the reader can come to terms with the multiple perspectives in Wilde's novel. This chapter examines the internal and external elements with an eye to discovering how they combine to influence individual approaches and produce unique and often unconventional readings.

The conclusion, chapter 7, focuses on "The Preface" to *The Picture of Dorian Gray,* looking at how Wilde tried to condition us to deal with different responses within a single work. It does not present a simple solution to this challenge. Rather, it shows how Wilde's writing confronts a tradition of linear thinking and encourages us to acknowledge multiple readings. In the end, this study reaffirms its central assumption (that the reader finally determines the meaning of the novel) by laying out methods of reading without using them to prescribe a particular meaning.

4

The Imaginative Response Invited by *The Picture of Dorian Gray*

What's in a name?

Romeo and Juliet

A man cannot be too careful in his choice of enemies.
The Picture of Dorian Gray

In Shakespeare's rhetorical question, one of the playwright's most famous characters sums up his response to the tension that arises from the clash of personal feelings and societal demands. Romeo's sweeping, dismissive gesture seeks to make the associations that adhere to any word—in this case, the hostility his relatives feel when they hear Juliet's surname, Capulet—irrelevant to our understanding of what the word signifies. In rejecting the proposition that the name Capulet can of itself make a person bad, however, he does more than signal a young man's determination to overcome the obstacles to love imposed by family loyalties. The consequences of the linguistic assumptions of his statement extend well beyond his immediate situation. One of those assumptions is that language has no power in and of itself to create meaning, that words function simply as arbitrary signs.

The second epigraph, taken from remarks made by Lord Henry Wotton in *The Picture of Dorian Gray*, adopts the very opposite approach to the question of the relationship between words and meaning. By recasting a tired observation on friendship, Lord Henry does more than shift its emphasis; he draws attention to how our expectations about language work both with and against specific declarations.

His remark about making enemies depends on the reader for its cleverness. If the reader does not recognize how Lord Henry's wit plays off conventional expectations, then the phrase loses its sharpness. For the reader sensitive to detail, however, Romeo's inclination to question the integrity of a particular word and Lord Henry's determination to overcome the predictability of an overused phrase offer interesting possibilities regarding the freedoms and restrictions encountered in any search for meaning in literature.

These contrasting individual responses to words are one illustration of the alternatives open to any reader. At the same time, recognizing his or her interpretive options is only the first step in a reader's movement toward a full understanding of the complex way any discourse functions. After Romeo's cavalier denial of the significance of Juliet's family—"What's in a name?"—he goes on, through analogy, to assert his belief in the stability of his perception of the thing itself—"that which we call a rose by any other name would smell as sweet" (2.2.42–43). With this declaration, Romeo confidently tells us that even though words may change, what we know remains constant. At the conclusion of the play, of course, Shakespeare demonstrates a far more sophisticated sense of how the balance between expectation and observation shapes meaning, and through this accommodation he suggests a more productive approach for his readers.

Likewise, Lord Henry's statement demonstrates not only how clichéd language can become fresh but also how what we anticipate enhances the meaning of the words we encounter. His remark shows us that even hackneyed expressions bring to mind certain associations that profoundly effect meaning, and the impact of his witticism comes largely from our expectation of a very different conclusion to his sentence. Like Shakespeare, Wilde recognizes the instability of language but also knows that words do not simply function as arbitrary signs. Unlike Lord Henry, whose wit depends on the easy inversion of what the listener expects, Wilde believes that every discourse can potentially convey several meanings. For the remainder of this chapter, I will examine how some elements in *The Picture of Dorian Gray* foster our sense that the novel can simultaneously support a number of very different meanings.

Of course, given the assurance that characterizes the statements of Lord Henry and Dorian, uncertainty may not seem at first glance a defining feature of the narrative descriptions the reader encounters in *The Picture of Dorian Gray*. Nonetheless, from the very beginning the novel's discourse offers contradictory signals about conventions. For example, the very title, *The Picture of Dorian Gray*, seems to unambiguously announce the central topic of the work. As the complexities of the narrative emerge, however, any certitude that the title initially inspires becomes less justified, and a range of alternative possibilities insistently begin to present themselves. In fact, the starkly definitive article *the* and the richly ambiguous noun *picture* do not so much define clear interpretive boundaries as mimic Romeo's expression of ambivalence by setting feelings of assurance and indecision in dynamic tension.

In its traditional grammatical function, *the* always establishes the presence of a single, clearly defined entity. In the context of the title of Wilde's novel, readers take its function to be the identification of a specific artistic rendition (*the* picture) of a particular figure (Dorian Gray) in a manner that sets it apart from and above all other pictures of that individual. The first word in the novel's title concentrates our attention on a particular object, elevating that object's stature.

The word that immediately follows, however—*picture*—works just as diligently to call into question the assumption that the subject is the definitive rendering of Dorian Gray. As a term that connotes an imaginative re-creation of the individual who served as its model, *picture* conveys a sense of far more subjectivity and hence far less stability than the reader might initially have assumed. This state of flux becomes more evident when the reader considers the implications of Wilde's decision to use the word *picture* rather than identify Basil

Hallward's creation by applying the apparently more precise designation *portrait*. The term *picture* offers a broad, nonprescriptive concept of representation, one that immediately opens up the possibility of a number of alternative perspectives. By contrast, *portrait* signifies a fairly specific and narrowly defined form of depiction, subject to very specific generic conventions.[1]

The *Oxford English Dictionary* offers several definitions that clearly underscore the markedly different meanings these two words carried for Wilde and his contemporaries, and these distinctions by and large remain in effect for modern readers. The *OED* turns to John Ruskin, one of Wilde's teachers at Oxford, for an illustration of the definition of *picture* as "representation as a work of art," quoting a passage from his *Arrows of Chace* (1852). "Every noble picture is a manuscript book, of which only one copy exists, or ever can exist." For the more specific sense of the term *portrait*, "a representation or delineation of a person, esp. of the face, made from life," the *OED* offers a range of Victorian views. Again turning to Ruskin, this time with a quotation from his book *Modern Painters* (1843), the *OED* underscores the position of portraiture as a subgenre of painting in the following example of its usage: "That habit of the old and great painters of introducing portrait into all their highest works." Giving an even more precise characterization of a portrait, the *OED* goes on to cite a passage from the London *Daily Chronicle* of 15 April 1904: "A very excellent portrait-study, a tender and loving reminiscence of the high-spirited . . . noble-hearted woman."

With these contemporary definitions before us, we can see how Wilde's decision to use the words *the* and *picture* to introduce the subject of his novel reflects the book's inclination to dispose readers toward a variety of possible responses. As it opens, the title seems to invite the reader to assume that the novel will present a definitive view of the character Dorian Gray. The word that follows, however, suggests that the narrative cannot avoid employing a subjective approach as part of its creative process: if indeed the painting of the title succeeds in depicting a particular individual, it does so only by transmitting his image through an intermediary, someone who re-presents a likeness of Dorian Gray through a picture. The act of painting itself, of course, requires the artist to commit to a particular perspective that directs the process of depiction. This necessity, however, does not resolve the issue of validity, for it begs the question of how valid the chosen point of view is in comparison with all the alternatives not selected.

This question is not readily clarified as the narrative unfolds. In fact, its features, if anything, reinforce the reader's growing sense that any of a number of equally valid yet diverse points of view can make a legitimate claim to being a genuine imaginative representation of Dorian Gray. Thus, the reader comes to the conclusion that *the* and *picture* introduce the contradictory impressions that will unite the aesthetic force of the narrative: on the one hand, the two words suggest that a single, primary interpretation of Dorian Gray (both the character and the novel) may exist, and on the other hand, they remind us that we construct any such interpretation out of a highly subjective response or series of responses.

Furthermore, in both its structure and content, Wilde's novel, a piece of prose describing the results of the act of painting, reminds us of the distance between the representations that appear in pictures and portraits and the written descriptions of those pictures and portraits. Just as the layers of sedimentation built up over centuries on a Renaissance painting can both enhance and obscure the original picture/portrait, the words that accumulate over the course of a novel's narrative can both illuminate and obscure the written picture/portrait. By the end of *The Picture of Dorian Gray*, these alternatives raise the question of just what the reader finds depicted in Wilde's novel. After comparing the complex psychological makeup of the discourse with the simplistic resolution on the final page, it no longer seems credible to view the novel simply as the realistic morality tale we may have thought we were reading, a modern parable that shows how evil is eventually punished. Instead, *The Picture of Dorian Gray* appears more like a palimpsest of multiple, equally compelling readings—a tablet used over and over again with traces of the earlier writing discernible between the lines of the most recent work.

Simply acknowledging that the narrative of *The Picture of Dorian Gray* can support multiple interpretations, however, does not resolve the problem of how to respond to the novel since anyone trying to come away with a unified impression still feels a fairly strong need to concentrate on one reading at a time. Thus, an obvious question arises after the novel seems to announce its subject as a very particular individual and then suggests that a number of different ways of perceiving that character are equally legitimate. If various people throughout the novel see Dorian differently, and if none of these points of view emerges immediately as the most accurate and logical one, which picture or point of view has the best claim to prominence? How the reader answers that question will, of course, shape his or her reading and interpretation of the rest of the novel. The reader should certainly survey the range of alternative perspectives of Dorian before deciding how to interpret the work as a whole.[2]

Perhaps the most direct source of our impressions of Dorian Gray's image is the artistic creation that moves the action of the story forward. Basil Hallward opens the novel by introducing to his friend Lord Henry Wotton—and to the readers—a painting of Dorian on which he has been working. Even in this apparently straightforward gesture, however, an enigmatic element emerges: "As the painter looked at the gracious and comely form he had so skilfully mirrored in his art, a smile of pleasure passed across his face, and seemed about to linger there. But he suddenly started up, and, closing his eyes, placed his fingers upon the lids, as though he sought to imprison within his brain some curious dream from which he feared he might awake" (1–2).

In Basil's apparent self-absorption before the picture and in Lord Henry's response, we get a clear sense of the powerful imaginative forces incorporated into its composition.

> "I know you will laugh at me," [Basil] replied, "but I really can't exhibit [the painting]. I have put too much of myself into it."
>
> "Too much of yourself into it! Upon my word, Basil, I didn't know you were so vain; and I really can't see any resemblance between you, with your rugged strong face and your coal-black hair, and this young Adonis, who looks as if he was made out of ivory and rose-leaves. Why, my dear Basil, he is a Narcissus, and you—well, of course you have an intellectual expression, and all

that. But beauty, real beauty, ends where an intellectual expression begins." (2–3)

Lord Henry's banter makes good-natured fun of Basil's statement. In doing so, however, Lord Henry uncharacteristically betrays himself as a superficial reader, for he reductively equates the self represented in the painting with the physical characteristics depicted. Basil, on the other hand, takes a more sophisticated view. He corrects Lord Henry's oversimplification and offers to both his friend and to us interpretive guidance regarding what constitutes a picture and what a picture reveals. He raises an important issue about the real subject of the painting when he goes on to say, "The reason I will not exhibit this picture is that I am afraid that I have shown in it the secret of my own soul" (5).

As the other characters offer their judgments of his work, it becomes increasingly clear to the reader that Basil's sense of seeing his self revealed in the painting reflects much more than mere egotism. His comments, like the reactions of both Dorian and Lord Henry, evoke the range of aesthetic effects open to all viewers of the picture, but also like them, he unconsciously reveals how much his own imagination works to create meaning in the painting. Dorian's response, for example, leaves little doubt as to the profound association he makes between himself and Basil's rendition: "When [Dorian] saw it he drew back, and his cheeks flushed for a moment with pleasure. A look of joy came into his eyes, as if he had recognized himself for the first time. . . . The sense of his own beauty came on him like a revelation" (24–25). And Lord Henry, though far less inclined than the others to project himself into the picture, makes its aesthetic essence part of his own consciousness. He sets himself up as the final judge of its merit and gives the painting a privileged position by declaring it "the finest portrait of modern times" (24).

The structure of the novel reinforces this impression of interpretive subjectivity, and by extension it shows how well Wilde understood how the individual imagination responds to a piece of art. The way the narrative evokes rather than describes Basil Hallward's painting gives readers the same inventive opportunities the characters have. We are not told what the painting looks like. Instead, as our imagination fills in the details of the work, it becomes our creation as much as Basil's, Lord Henry's, or Dorian's.

In a succession of powerful scenes, the novel heightens this association between art and the individual imagination. As the narrative traces the psychological changes in Dorian's nature, it makes both the young man and the reader aware that the picture exercises a kinetic rather than static influence on the process. After Dorian's bitter exchange with Sybil Vane and the long night he spends walking about the city, for example, he returns home at daybreak and notices his portrait. "In the dim arrested light that struggled through the cream-coloured silk blinds, the face appeared to him to be a little changed. The expression looked different. One would have said that there was a touch of cruelty in the mouth. It was certainly strange" (89–90).

As Dorian's nature coarsens, the transformation of the picture continues. As a result, the reader's imagination must continually reconstruct the painting to keep pace with the narrative cues marking its degradation. At first, the discourse records relatively minor changes, distinguishable to only the most discerning viewer. "Was the face on the canvas viler than before? . . . Gold hair, blue eyes, and rose-red lips—they were all there. It was simply the expression that had altered. That was horrible in its cruelty" (119). Later, however, the process accelerates, and the reader's need to change his or her imaginative sense of the painting becomes even more compelling as Dorian compares the picture with his own countenance.

> He himself would . . . stand, with a mirror, in front of the portrait . . . looking now at the evil and aging face on the canvas, and now at the fair young face that laughed back at him from the polished glass. (128)

> It was true that the portrait still preserved, under all the foulness and ugliness of the face, its marked likeness to himself. (141)

Although the picture undergoes undeniable alterations, the overall degeneration resists easy classification, for it occurs gradually in the mind of each reader whose imagination participates in its refashioning.

As the novel moves toward its conclusion, references to the corruption of the picture proliferate. When Basil Hallward inspects his radically changed painting just before Dorian murders him, the discourse underscores a general abhorrence. At the same time, it makes no attempt to give specific details. "[Basil] held the light up again to the canvas, and examined it. The surface seemed to be quite undisturbed, and as he had left it. It was from within, apparently, that the foulness and horror had come. Through some strange quickening of inner life the leprosies of sin were slowly eating the thing away. The rotting of a corpse in a watery grave was not so fearful" (157). Wilde's narrative strategy, in fact, is to actively resist a definitive description of the picture's condition. Instead, as evidenced in the quotation above, the picture is discussed on a general level that in effect invites readers to fill in the details.

Even the grotesqueness of the portrait, however, becomes monotonous after a while; to sustain the multiple perspectives, Wilde takes care to remind us how beautiful the picture remains in the recollections of some. For example, in his last meeting with Dorian, Lord Henry, fondly recalls the painting as the crowning achievement of Basil's career. "It was really a masterpiece. I remember I wanted to buy it. I wish I had now. It belonged to Basil's best period" (214). Wilde goes on to highlight the variety of images constituting the novel's representation of the picture by deftly contrasting this nostalgic impression with the rage Dorian feels when he views the portrait privately a few moments later and sees that his putative good act—resisting the temptation to seduce Hetty Merton—had no effect on the painting. "A cry of pain and indignation broke from him. He could see no change, save that in the eyes there was a look of cunning, and in the mouth the curved wrinkle of the hypocrite. The thing was still loathsome—more loathsome, if possible, than before—and the scarlet dew that spotted the hand seemed brighter, and more like blood newly spilt" (221).

As powerful as this description may be, Wilde does not allow it to resolve unambiguously the question of the nature of the painting; he does not give readers this grotesque image as their last view of the degenerated picture. Instead, he moves the pattern of perception back to the portrait as it appeared originally. When, immediately following Dorian's death, his servants burst into the attic schoolroom where the picture has been kept for years, they find the images exactly reversed. Wilde uses a final comparison of Dorian and his representation to enforce upon our minds the enduring question of which representation throughout the work actually embodies Dorian. "When they entered, they found hanging upon the wall a splendid portrait of their master as they had last seen him, in all the wonder of his exquisite youth and beauty. Lying on the floor was a dead man, in evening dress, with a knife in his heart. He was withered, wrinkled, and loathsome of visage. It was not till they had examined the rings that they recognized who it was" (224).

The picture is only one element of the novel that stimulates multiple meanings; Dorian's own nature serves as a much more complex but no less effective vehicle for evoking different points of view. Basil Hallward, Lord Henry, and Dorian himself offer highly personal and equally evocative impressions of the young man. Unlike descriptions of the painting, however, their views are presented in direct terms that prove far less susceptible to modification by the reader's imagination.

Despite their highly subjective slants, each perspective offers useful insights that help form a unified conception of Dorian's nature. Hallward's description of the feelings aroused by his friend, for example, shakes up some assumptions the reader may have made about Dorian's nature. For instance, Basil characterizes his first meeting with Dorian in the tender terms a lover might use:

> I suddenly became conscious that some one was looking at me. I turned half-way round, and saw Dorian Gray for the first time. When our eyes met, I felt that I was growing pale. A curious sensation of terror came over me. I knew that I had come face to face with some one whose mere personality was so fascinating that, if I allowed it to do so, it would absorb my whole nature, my whole soul, my very art itself. . . . Something seemed to tell me that I was on the verge of a terrible crisis in my life. I had a strange feeling that Fate had in store for me exquisite joys and exquisite sorrows. (6)

Despite certain obvious parallels between this description and various conventions of romantic love, Basil's interest in Dorian proves to be far more complex than frank homoerotic desire.[3] Basil, in fact, finds Dorian a source of artistic fulfillment—as an inspiration—rather than an object of physical gratification.

> The mere visible presence of this lad . . . defines for me the lines of a fresh school, a school that is to have in it all the passion of the romantic spirit, all the perfection of the spirit that is Greek. . . . Dorian Gray is to me simply a motive in art. You might see nothing in him. I see everything in him. He is never more present in my work than when no image of him is there. He is a suggestion, as I have said, of a new manner. I find him in the curves of certain lines, in the loveliness and subtleties of certain colours. (10–11)

Basil's focus on Dorian's power to provoke an aesthetic response should not, of course, distract the reader's attention from the effect on the artist of the young man's physical charm. Basil's response as an artist does, however, remind us that conceptions of Dorian the person run parallel to reactions to his depiction in the painting: impressions of Dorian depend as much on the imaginative response of the viewer as on his actual features. Thus, when Lord Henry draws Dorian away from the painter for a night at the theater, we can understand what Basil means when he declares his intention to "stay with the real Dorian" (29). The painter refers not so much to the portrait he has just completed as to the unblemished image of Dorian he retains in his mind.

As noted above, Wilde cannot use the attitudes of his characters to elicit a range of reader responses in the same way he uses the painting. Nonetheless, he does employ his characters' opinions to demonstrate the limitations that arise when an individual's imaginative response becomes fixed and no longer subject to the ongoing process of revision. The flaw in Basil's view, for example, derives not from his preference for his intellectual portrait of Dorian over all others but from his having allowed his mental picture to become static, a condition his painting in fact has resisted.

Dorian's initial innocence makes such an impression on Basil that throughout his life the painter literally cannot see Dorian any other way. Just as Dorian's youthful nature inspired his best painting, he assumes that it continues—unsullied—to inspire the best in everyone Dorian encounters.[4]

Having allowed his first impression to calcify into a static, prescriptive view, Basil shows remarkable tenacity in the face of evidence that would surely shift the opinion of a less devoted friend. Basil does not, of course, remain indifferent to the growing callousness he sees in Dorian, especially after the death of Sybil Vane: "Dorian, this is horrible! Something has changed you completely. You look exactly the same wonderful boy who, day after day, sued to come down to my studio to sit for his picture. But you were simple, natural, and affectionate then. You were the most unspoiled creature in the whole world. Now, I don't know what has come over you. You talk as if you had no heart, no pity in you. It is all Harry's influence. I see that" (108).

Nonetheless, as he listens to Dorian's simple response—"I am what I am. There is nothing more to be said" (110)—Basil essentially admits that he is no longer capable of critically assessing his subject. Instead, he drops his probing tone and reverts to his initial view of Dorian: "The painter felt strangely moved. The lad was infinitely dear to him, and his personality had been the great turning-point in his art. He could not bear the idea of reproaching him any more. After all, his indifference was probably merely a mood that would pass away. There was so much in him that was good, so much in him that was noble" (110).

Even as Basil reiterates his commitment to a single view of Dorian, the narrative continues to underscore the pluralism that runs throughout the discourse. Basil's impression of his friend never significantly changes, but his sensitivity to public opinion keeps the reader aware of these contrasting views of Dorian: "I think it right that you should know that the most dreadful things are being said against you in London. . . . Mind you, I don't believe these rumours at all. At least, I can't believe them when I see you. Sin is a thing that writes itself across a man's face. It cannot be concealed" (149). Despite the terrible stories of Dorian's depravity, Basil begs his friend to give him some reason to sustain his vision of the unsullied young man he once knew: "You must give me some answer to these horrible charges that are made against you. If you tell me that they are absolutely untrue from beginning to end, I shall believe you. Deny them, Dorian, deny them! Can't you see what I am going through? My God! don't tell me that you are bad, and corrupt, and shameful" (154). Indeed, when confronted with incontrovertible evidence—the once beautiful painting transformed into a disfigured icon, emblematic of Dorian's degraded nature—Basil still refuses to relinquish his vision of Dorian's earlier state or his belief that it could be regained. "It is never too late, Dorian. Let us kneel down and try if we cannot remember a prayer. Isn't there a verse somewhere, 'Though your sins be as scarlet, yet I will make them as white as snow'?" (158).

These final sentiments say much more about Basil's nature than about Dorian's. Nevertheless, the painter's tenacity in retaining his original opinion of the young man provides an object lesson to readers: despite the fallacies we see in Basil's argument, we cannot avoid being reminded by it of how Dorian appeared at the novel's opening. No matter how Dorian has changed, the person he becomes evolved from that earlier figure, and Basil's initial impression remains an important part of not only Basil's but the reader's sense of him. Thus, just as Basil foolishly tries to exclude Dorian's present behavior from a picture of him, the reader is equally benighted in trying to ignore his past.

With a self-confidence that surpasses even Basil's faith in his ability to discern the true nature of Dorian, Lord Henry Wotton also has his own imaginative construction of Dorian, one he reiterates throughout the novel and relies on as a gauge for assessing his friend's behavior. While his perspective on Dorian is undeniably different from Basil's, Lord Henry's appraisal parallels the painter's in several key areas. Specifically, Lord Henry's conception of his friend rests solely on assumptions formed at his earliest meeting with Dorian, and with only minor modifications, his opinions remain steadfastly true to those early impressions. Nonetheless, despite their rigidity, Lord Henry's attitudes offer readers useful insights into Dorian's nature.

Like Basil's first assessment, Lord Henry's initial response to Dorian underscores the powerful effect of the young man's physical beauty and spiritual innocence: "Lord Henry looked at him. Yes, he was certainly wonderfully handsome, with his finely-curved scarlet lips, his frank blue eyes, his crisp gold hair. There was something in his face that made one trust him at once. All the candour of youth was there, was well as all youth's passionate purity. One felt that he had kept himself unspotted from the world" (15). Of far greater significance, however, is how each man, in his reaction to Dorian, develops further impressions from this initial recognition of physical perfection. To Basil, Dorian's beauty signifies goodness and is an inspiration to his art. Lord Henry, on the other hand, makes a direct connection between Dorian's youthful charm and his emotional inexperience. He anticipates the changes Dorian's nature will undergo, a prospect he views as a wonderful chance to observe human development. Lord Henry's views raise an important point: even at this early stage in the narrative, he has begun to shift our attention from an exclusive concern with Dorian's physical attractiveness and encouraged us to take note of his moral nature.

Basil, of course, has also given consideration to Dorian's character, but he assesses it less rigorously and more idealistically. He sees Dorian's beauty quite simply as a testament to his goodness. This equation commits Basil to taking a fairly simplistic approach to judging his friend's integrity: as long as that beauty endures, Basil remains a steadfast defender of Dorian's honor. Lord Henry, on the other hand, sees a more dynamic relationship between beauty and morality—as he tells Dorian in a passage that redefines conventional conceptions of principled behavior.

> Ah! realize your youth while you have it. Don't squander the gold of your days, listening to the tedious, trying to improve the hopeless failure, or giving away your life to the ignorant, the common, and the vulgar. These are the sickly aims, the false ideals, of our age. Live! Live the wonderful life that is in you! Let nothing be lost upon you. Be always searching for new sensations. Be afraid of nothing. . . . [Wilde's ellipses] A new Hedonism—that is what our century wants. (22)

As *The Picture of Dorian Gray* progresses, this view increasingly distinguishes Lord Henry's perception of Dorian from Basil's.

In fact, from a very early point in the novel, Lord Henry counters Basil's idealized picture by drawing both Dorian's and the reader's attention to the powerful force of sensual desire inherent in the young man's nature: "You, Mr. Gray, you yourself, with your rose-red youth and your rose-white boyhood, you have had passions that have made you afraid, thoughts that have filled you with terror, day-dreams and sleeping dreams whose mere memory might stain your cheek with shame" (18). The floral metaphors Lord Henry uses to describe Dorian's present condition—"your rose-red youth and your rose-white boyhood"—take on a dual function. They enforce the fragile, temporary nature of Dorian's beauty. (These descriptions may also evoke the fairy-tale figures Snow White and Rose Red, images of femininity and fantasy that may further complicate readers' impressions.) And by linking the description of the effect of Dorian's imagination with references to his physical attractiveness, Lord Henry reshapes the relationship between beauty and goodness that Basil articulates. Basil wishes to affirm that good looks testify to purity. Lord Henry looks at the same phenomenon from the opposite perspective: fading beauty serves as a sign of decadence. This harsher view of physical appearance as a measure of moral development, implied but never articulated by Basil, is foregrounded in Lord Henry's attitude that degeneration is the inevitable price of self-indulgence.

Thus, Lord Henry can frankly acknowledge Dorian's beauty as both powerful and temporary, for its very transitory quality endows it with a force Lord Henry understands only too well. "You have a wonderfully beautiful face, Mr. Gray. . . . And Beauty is a form of Genius—is higher, indeed, than Genius, as it needs no explanation. It is one of the great facts of the world, like sunlight, or spring-time, or the reflection in dark waters of that silver shell we call the moon. It cannot be questioned. It has its divine right of sovereignty. It makes princes of those who have it" (21). Lord Henry emphasizes a carpe diem view. As noted above, he calls his philosophy New Hedonism, which he presents not as a way to forestall aging and decay but as a way to make the most of the brief time one has before physical degeneration sets in. From this point of view, the scenario of Dorian's life has a fatalistic inevitability. Because his beauty—his "form of Genius"—is great, Dorian will suffer greatly when his beauty disappears. The New Hedonism Lord Henry offers as a response to his predicament will allow Dorian to build a recollection of pleasures to offer bittersweet consolation when aging inevitably takes its toll on his attractiveness.

Lord Henry's own life attests to the potential allure of such cerebral, voyeuristic pleasures. Indeed, as he outlines his impressions of Dorian, Lord Henry relegates beauty to a secondary role and emphasizes that the ambivalences in Dorian's nature and the possibility of shaping Dorian's consciousness combine to attract him.

> And how charming [Dorian] had been at dinner the night before, as with startled eyes and lips parted in frightened pleasure he had sat opposite to him at the club, the red candleshades staining to a richer rose the wakening wonder of his face. Talking to him was like playing upon an exquisite violin. He answered to every touch and thrill of the bow. . . . There was nothing [Lord Henry] could not do with [Dorian]. He could be made a Titan or a toy. What a pity it was that such beauty was destined to fade. (35–36)

In fact, despite his regret over the effect time will have on Dorian's attractiveness, Lord Henry's intellectual curiosity and powers of observation provide a measure of self-consolation. Dorian's inner nature as much as his beauty fascinates Lord Henry, who has a sharp eye for psychological development. Scarcely a month after meeting Dorian, he takes pleasure in noting the contrast between the young man's earlier demeanor and his current appearance: "How different he was now from the shy, frightened boy he had met in Basil Hallward's studio! His nature had developed like a flower, had borne blossoms of scarlet flame. Out of its secret hiding-place had crept his Soul, and Desire had come to meet it on the way" (54–55).

This absorption with the transformation of Dorian's psyche is a continuing source of satisfaction for Lord Henry and the feature distinguishing his perspective on the younger man. He all but admits as much to Basil in the comment he makes after learning of Dorian's engagement to Sybil Vane: "I hope that Dorian Gray will make this girl his wife, passionately adore her for six months, and then suddenly become fascinated by some one else. He would be a wonderful study" (74).

Indeed, Basil's genuine concern for his friend contrasts sharply with Lord Henry's voyeuristic view of Dorian. Though much affected by Dorian's physical presence, as the younger man's friend Basil takes his beauty for granted. He nonetheless worries a great deal about Dorian's goodness. Lord Henry, on the other hand, feels no interest in Dorian's nature stronger than curiosity, and even that interest relates directly to the pleasure he derives from observation. At the same time, he retains a deep involvement with Dorian's appearance— as is clearly evidenced in his efforts to console Dorian after the death of Sybil Vane. "Life has everything in store for you, Dorian. There is nothing that you, with your extraordinary good looks, will not be able to do. . . . [Y]ou must keep your good looks. We live in an age that reads too much to be wise and that thinks too much to be beautiful. We cannot spare you" (104).

Certain key features of Lord Henry's relationship with Dorian do in fact parallel Basil's. Specifically, as the novel unfolds and the picture begins to change, Lord Henry loses access to Dorian's innermost thoughts. Indeed, the transformations of both Dorian's body (with the picture serving as proxy) and his soul are secrets he will share with no one. More surprisingly, however, both Basil and Lord Henry retain a fairly rigid, unchanging sense of their friend. Just as Basil always looks on Dorian as the beautiful companion whose purity inspires his art, Lord Henry continues to see Dorian as the precocious pupil whose sophistication and worldliness remain at the level of the tutelage he gave Dorian after the death of Sybil Vane. Lord Henry seems totally unaware that changes are taking place.

As the novel moves toward its conclusion, Lord Henry's view of Dorian—in its own way as idealized as Basil's—counterpoints the brutal impressions the young man's actions have made on readers. "You have everything in the world that a man can want. There is no one who would not be delighted to change places with you" (203–4). As ironic as those lines may seem to us, Lord Henry's continuing fascination with his friend reminds us of the power of the young man's attractiveness and charm to shape people's impressions, and these attributes set themselves against any revulsion we feel toward Dorian's nature. "You [Dorian] are the type of what the age is searching for, and what it is afraid it has found. I am so glad that you have never done anything, never carved a statue, or painted a picture, or produced anything outside of yourself! Life has been your art. You have set yourself to music. Your days are your sonnets" (217).

Complementing these highly impressionistic views, Dorian also offers a representation of himself that seems no less subjective, nor at the same time any less convincing, than those of the others. In many ways, in fact, Dorian's self-assessment, at least initially, echoes the impressions already articulated by his friends. When, for example, Lord Henry suggests that Dorian experiences an imaginative life far less placid than his demeanor would lead one to expect, Dorian silently affirms that view: "Yes; there had been things in his boyhood that he had not understood. He understood them now. Life suddenly became fiery-coloured to him. It seemed to him that he had been walking in fire. Why had he not known it?" (19). With this newfound understanding comes a sense of his own mortality every bit as intense as that felt by Lord Henry. "How sad it is! I shall grow old, and horrible, and dreadful. But this picture will remain always young. . . . Lord Henry Wotton is perfectly right. Youth is the only thing worth having. When I find that I am growing old, I shall kill myself" (25–26).

As the narrative unfolds, Dorian gains a great deal of worldly experience and confidence that seem to relegate such thoughts of self-destruction to the immaturity of his youth. Nonetheless, he remains susceptible to external influences. Basil quickly loses any ability to sway Dorian's feelings. On the other hand, Lord Henry, as we see in his conversation with Dorian after the death of Sybil Vane, remains adept at illuminating Dorian's sense of himself. More significantly, however, the painting becomes an increasingly prominent force in Dorian's life. "As he often remembered afterwards, and always with no small wonder, he found himself at first gazing at the portrait with a feeling of almost scientific interest. That such a change should have taken place was incredible to him. And yet it was a fact. . . . He shuddered, and felt afraid, and, going back to the couch, lay there, gazing at the picture in sickened horror" (95).

The painting brings out the paradoxical attitudes at work in Dorian's consciousness, for it exerts both a liberating and an inhibiting effect. On the one hand, the picture gives him the advantage of escaping the horror he would have to face if his body began to show the physical consequences of the growing depravity of his life. At the same time, the demeanor of the portrait reminds him, with unrelenting insistence, of the inescapable effects of his debauchery. Of course, because his body does not suffer the physical ravages such a life would inflict on others, there seems to be no material reason for him to resist the temptation to indulge in even greater excesses. Nonetheless, the painting does have a psychological impact by constantly rebuking his behavior and, by extension, calling into question the fundamental validity of the philosophy of New Hedonism.

Thus, the picture confronts Dorian's sensibilities with an awareness of guilt and shame that he cannot easily escape, and his periodic admissions of the impact of these feelings—even in the most incongruous of situations—impress upon us the complexities of his nature. "The presence of Adrian Singleton [in the opium den] troubled [Dorian]. He wanted to be where no one would know who he was. He wanted to escape from himself" (188). Coming after a series of vacillations—his temporary remorse over the death of Sybil Vane, his resentment over Basil's determination to see him as a character capable of repentance, his genuine sorrow over the necessity of blackmailing Alan Campbell—a scene like this sets Dorian apart from the stereotypical sensualist and suggests a range of ambivalences in his nature.

In the final pages of Wilde's novel, the spiritual callousness that had previously shielded Dorian, like the picture itself, seems to give way under the pressure of an obsessive sense of guilt.

> Was it really true that one could never change? He felt a wild longing for the unstained purity of his boyhood—his rose-white boyhood, as Lord Henry had once called it. He knew that he had tarnished himself, filled his mind with corruption and given horror to his fancy; that he had been an evil influence to others, and had experienced a terrible joy in being so; and that of the lives that had crossed his own it had been the fairest and the most full

of promise that he had brought to shame. But was it all irretrievable? Was there no hope for him? (219–20)

At this point, the narrative threatens to decline into sentimental melodrama. It is arguable, however, that the narrative needs to project such a tone to prepare the reader for the enormity of the self-loathing that has become part of Dorian's nature, as the reader witnesses in his last look at the painting: "He went in quietly . . . and dragged the purple hanging from the portrait. A cry of pain and indignation broke from him. The thing was still loathsome—more loathsome, if possible, than before" (221).

Dorian's inability to sustain the range of different pictures of himself, his ultimately irresistible need for closure and certitude, marks the failure of his imagination—the one flaw Lord Henry's code of New Hedonism cannot tolerate. The melodramatic conclusion to the novel—one that Dorian himself would surely abhor—is his punishment for failing to sustain his own innovative power. He becomes an example for the reader, who must work to avoid the reductiveness that ultimately proves so costly to Dorian.

Each of these perspectives—Basil Hallward's, Lord Henry's, Dorian Gray's, and even that of the picture itself—offers a very poignant and powerful view of the nature of Dorian Gray, and each arguably suggests a valid estimation of his character. Of course, for the reader attempting to formulate his or her own image of Dorian Gray, the very validity of all these different points of view raises a range of potential problems. They remind the reader of the insufficiency of an approach to interpretation that relies on any single attitude to depict fully the nature of Dorian. Thus, the question that arises is not so much whether the reader constructs his or her own picture of Dorian Gray independently or adopts the perspective of one of the central characters, but whether alternatives exist to the exclusionary approaches followed by Basil, Lord Henry, and Dorian himself.

To some degree, the picture itself offers a useful model for viewing Dorian. Its changing features remind us of the kinetic qualities of both Dorian's character and the interpretive process. At the same time, a certain inevitability limits the picture's alternatives: the image of Dorian goes through progressive stages of degeneration with little or no allowance for variation. Its inadequacy, like the weaknesses in the other renderings of Dorian, points toward the need to adopt an interpretive approach that goes beyond the deterministic certitude of a single point of view. *The Picture of Dorian Gray*, from the ironic definitiveness of its title to the artificial closure of its final lines, invites a broader, freer response. As I noted at the beginning of this chapter, the novel's title seems to declare an intention to offer an authoritative rendering of the central character, yet by making no single perspective of Dorian sufficient, the novel clearly returns that task to the reader and invites him or her to form an amalgamated image from the different alternatives offered in the narrative.

Acknowledging this challenge does not mean that the reader must dilute or synthesize these different versions of Dorian into yet another perspective; such a requirement would imply the possibility of eventually imposing a single meaning, a possibility the structure of the novel does not sustain. *The Picture of Dorian Gray* works against any easy resolution, including one based on the amalgamation of its differing perspectives. Thus, the force of the title lies not so much in its identification of a single representation of Dorian Gray as in its subtle characterization of the picture as continually changing but retaining within it a variety of images of Dorian—given varying emphases—that form one's total impression.

This is the approach I develop in subsequent chapters: while these diverse pictures of Dorian Gray are not necessarily mutually exclusive, they do resist the impulse toward integration. The reader may accept any one of them without being hampered from seeing the logic of another, but he or she does not thereby acquire the means to reconcile the diversities into a single dominant feature. In fact, the reader can maintain a number of different pictures in Wilde's novel simultaneously without stratifying or synthesizing them.

5

Ethics and Aesthetics

It is better to be beautiful than to be good. . . . But it is better to be good than to be ugly.

The Picture of Dorian Gray

Chapter 4 introduced an approach to reading *The Picture of Dorian Gray* that might seem to invert the usual pattern of exposition. It began by outlining reasons for resisting conventional attempts to impose definitive answers on all the questions raised by the narrative. Then it identified a range of possibilities for determining meaning before going on to acknowledge that they all represent equally valid responses. At first glance, the reader might feel tempted to dismiss this method as an invitation to interpretive anarchy. In fact, accepting the idea that the narrative of *The Picture of Dorian Gray* can produce a number of equally acceptable reactions without causing chaos reflects a logical extension of common habits of reading.

Since our encounter with Dick and Jane chasing their dog Spot across the pages of our first-grade primer, we have not been innocent or unencumbered readers. We bring to each successive work expectations based on our reactions to everything else we have already read. Each individual's reading experience remains unique, yet it also grows out of a collective cultural heritage that puts our responses in a broader context.

Thus, we approach *The Picture of Dorian Gray* aware of the many different readings it can inspire but at the same time expecting to build our interpretations on a foundation of common understanding. That is to say, any two individuals may find contrasting meanings in a piece of fiction, but we all base our interpretive efforts, in part at least, on certain shared values. We also accept the validity of the intellectual tradition of developing insights through open discussion of differing interpretive opinions. To facilitate such discussions, we rely on those shared values to provide the stability for the exchange of wide-ranging responses.

Most often, such shared values help readers identify the generally accepted limits on ordinary behavior that govern conduct in any society. Since much of our interpretive energy goes into assessing the actions of fictional characters, those commonly agreed upon boundaries then become the basis for any effort to generate meaning from the text. An ethical commonplace, like Socrates' pronouncement that "the unexamined life is not worth living," can illustrate how both individual readings and common values combine to form a meaningful response to *The Picture of Dorian Gray*.

On the immediate interpretive level, Socrates' adage sums up the thematic premise that gives the narrative of *The Picture of Dorian Gray* its structure: the novel progresses through a series of scenes that focus attention on how Dorian, his friends, and readers themselves assess the relationship between events and the shape of their lives. Comprehension of their actions, however, depends on an awareness of the values shared by the characters, the author, and the readers that serve as the standard for gauging behavior. Acknowledging the close association in any response to a piece of art between individual interpretive judgment and general moral convictions—the link between aesthetics and ethics—is a sound approach not simply for understanding the nature of Dorian and other characters but also for coming to grips with the meaning of the whole work.[1]

Much like the other formal features of *The Picture of Dorian Gray*, its ethical elements play off the reader's individual response to encourage multiple points of view within the narrative. At the same time, the ethical elements serve as important deterrents to any inclination toward relativism that such breadth of interpretation might at first seem to condone. As this chapter demonstrates, the moral components of the novel evoke those common values familiar to every reader, providing intellectual stability across a broad spectrum of interpretive responses.[2]

Understanding how alternative ways of reading can function within reasonable boundaries, however, calls for a bit of background, particularly if we are to be able to identify the cultural assumptions that shape the general understanding we bring to the ethical-aesthetic relationship depicted in *The Picture of Dorian Gray*. To begin with, we must trace the connections between the personal suppositions, both moral and artistic, of contemporary readers and the tradition of Western thought linking ethical and aesthetic concerns that has evolved over centuries of intellectual inquiry.[3] Wilde, of course, studied this tradition as a classics scholar at Oxford, and not surprisingly, we find in the Greek tradition of moral philosophy an important influence on the ethical-aesthetic features of *The Picture of Dorian Gray*.[4]

Such an overview necessarily begins with the discourses of Socrates. They underscore our society's long tradition of affirming the ideal of right conduct, and they offer a glimpse of early efforts to discover, articulate, and reconcile the moral tenets that guide us, the process of fashioning our behavior to fit our beliefs. Plato extended these ideals beyond the Socratic concern with the relationship between action and immediate material gain. He took up the examination of a system—designated by the term "ethics"—that functions as a means to goodness and that sees goodness as a means to happiness.

In surveying the views of subsequent philosophers, however, it becomes apparent that the Greeks did not in fact exhaust the limits of useful inquiry in this field. Aristotle saw ethics as the science of right conduct but took that idea no further. He sought to clarify his views in *Nicomachean Ethics* through a rigorous analysis of the attributes considered virtuous and through his articulation of the "golden mean," the middle ground between extremes of behavior. Unlike Plato, he did not see goodness as a means to happiness. For him, happiness was activity—specifically, activity in accordance with virtue.

Over the next thousand years, the debate over whether goodness leads to happiness remained a central philosophical question. From the disputations of the Stoics to the writings of Saint Augustine, on through the teachings of the Scholastics (especially Saint Thomas Aquinas), and then in the views of the humanists, the debate continued as to whether goodness produces happiness. During the Renaissance, however, in the works of thinkers as diverse as Niccolò Machiavelli, Martin Luther, and Thomas Hobbes, a series of pragmatic alternatives arose to challenge the implicit idealism of traditional disputations about ethical conduct. (Perhaps the cynicism of such writers as Machiavelli was a predictable reaction to the views of the Christian philosophers who linked ethical behavior as much to the avoidance of guilt as to the pursuit of happiness.)

In the eighteenth century, Immanuel Kant asserted the importance of doing right simply for its own sake and apart from self-interested motivations. During the same period, David Hume observed in his writings that a growing sense of the subjectivity of ethical endeavors had become an explicit part of the discourse. In the nineteenth century, Jeremy Bentham and other utilitarians advanced, even more emphatically than did Hume, a pragmatic ethics that seemed to reject abstract standards of behavior.[5]

Despite this fluctuation over the course of two and a half millennia of the status of ethics in the social consciousness, no one mounted a sustained and convincing argument against its indisputable presence. Even the arch-sensualist of *The Picture of Dorian Gray*, Lord Henry Wotton, does not reject ethics but rather seeks to redefine received opinions through an alternative system: "A new Hedonism—that is what our century wants" (22).[6]

The overall constancy of ethics notwithstanding, the relatively recent view of it as a personal code, advanced since the eighteenth-century Enlightenment, stands as an important transitional concept. The introduction of this point of view laid the groundwork for the perspective that would ultimately characterize Wilde's idea of the relationship between art and morality. Specifically, the contention that individuals can maintain a personal system of ethics paved the way for the development of mid-nineteenth-century aesthetic attitudes like those of the Pre-Raphaelite Brotherhood. Once the possibility of diverse moral systems is accepted, it becomes relatively easy to see the validity of a range of aesthetic views: if at heart our moral system admits a personal bias (no matter how small), then attempts to restrict value judgments of lesser significance, like those relating to aesthetics, are ludicrous.

Buoyed by this critical latitude, the Pre-Raphaelites rejected the previous century's artistic conventions, which they saw as designed to heighten the effect of a work through artifice. Instead, they committed themselves to the identification and representation of truthfulness and simplicity, often reflected in their devotion to nature. Furthermore, they took the position that artworks have value as ends in themselves rather than as means to separate goals. The Pre-Raphaelites provided the intellectual basis for the view of art as aesthetically and ethically self-contained, summed up in the single phrase—art for art's sake—that served as an informal motto of the loosely defined, late-nineteenth-century Aesthetic Movement.

Introduced and championed in France by Théophile Gautier, Charles Baudelaire, Gustave Flaubert, and Stéphane Mallarmé, the Aesthetic Movement found an able English spokesman in Walter Pater. All these men subscribed to the doctrine that art represents the supreme value because it is self-sufficient and has no aim beyond its own perfection. They asserted that the function of a work of art lies simply in its existence and in its ability to exude beauty, and that art is indifferent to the reigning social values.

This proposition advanced a crucial redefinition of the relationship between art and morality, and it provides an important perspective on *The Picture of Dorian Gray*, a work many judged as a prime example of art-for-art's-sake aesthetics. At first glance, the Aesthetic Movement's ideas may seem a direct rejection of morality in favor of pleasure, but in fact they encompassed a far more complex view of the relationship between the two. Rather than denying a place for ethics within an aesthetic experience, the Aesthetic Movement denied the primacy of conventional value systems and bluntly asserted the validity of alternative moralities. Thus, the idea discussed in chapter 4 of multiple perspectives as embodied in individual characters is also present in the ethical and aesthetic elements of the novel and, from another perspective, even in the aesthetics of the society from which it emerged.

While England was still absorbing this new interpretation, in France artistic attitudes continued to evolve beyond it. There the Aesthetic Movement gave way to the Decadents, who held that art occupies a position totally opposed to nature, in both senses of the word—nature as a physical force of biological change and nature as a metaphysical condition presenting standards of morality. In place of the heightened sensitivity of the Pre-Raphaelites, artists like Arthur Rimbaud advocated "the systematic derangement of all senses." With a self-conscious and restless curiosity, the Decadents asserted art's supremacy over nature, and they attacked accepted standards by adopting overrefined sensibilities and by aggressively perverting conventions. It was against this backdrop that Wilde offered his rendering of the relationship between art and morality in *The Picture of Dorian Gray.*

It is important to note that there is no easy correlation between Wilde's work and contemporaneous Continental aesthetic-ethical dispositions. The 1895 trials that eventually led to Wilde's incarceration at hard labor for two years may have associated him and his art in the popular imagination with decadence and the Decadent Movement. In fact, his imaginative concerns were with issues less sensational yet far more sophisticated. Specifically, the Aesthetic Movement—and in particular the views of Walter Pater as articulated in *Studies in the History of the Renaissance* (1873), later simply called *The Renaissance,* which set rigorous yet unconventional creative standards—allowed Wilde to introduce multiple points of view that went beyond narrow moral concerns without succumbing to the extravagant nihilism of the Decadents.[6]

Part of the appeal of Pater's views for someone of Wilde's sensibilities would have been the grounding of those views in an acknowledged—if somewhat idiosyncratic—system of ethical values. Despite the aura of moral depravity that the concept of art for art's sake suggested to some, Pater's advocacy of the idea was not accompanied by an abandonment of principled behavior, as Wilde surely knew. As the famous conclusion to *The Renaissance* demonstrates, Pater's position offers not an alternative but rather a new approach to ethical-aesthetic thinking.

Philosophiren, says Novalis, *ist dephlegmatisiren vivificiren* [To philosophize is to cast off inertia, to vitalize]. The service of philosophy, of speculative culture, towards the human spirit, is to rouse, to startle it to a life of constant and eager observation. Every moment some form grows perfect in hand or face; some tone on the hills or the sea is choicer than the rest; some mood of passion or insight or intellectual excitement is irresistibly real and attractive to us,—for that moment only. Not the fruit of experience, but experience itself, is the end. A counted number of pulses only is given to us of a variegated dramatic life. How may we see in them all that is to be seen in them by the finest senses? How shall we pass most swiftly from point to point, and be present always at the focus where the greater number of vital forces unite in their purest energy?

To burn always with this hard, gemlike flame, to maintain this ecstasy, is success in life. In a sense it might even be said that our failure is to form habits: for, after all, habit is relative to a stereotyped world, and meantime it is only the roughness of the eye that makes any two persons, things, situations, seem alike. While all melts under our feet, we may well grasp at any exquisite passion, or any contribution to knowledge that seems by a lifted horizon to set the spirit free for a moment, or any stirring of the senses, strange dyes, strange colours, and curious odours, or work of the artist's hands, or the face of one's friend. Not to discriminate in every moment some passionate attitude in those about us, and in the very brilliancy of their gifts some tragic dividing of forces on their ways, is, on this short day of frost and sun, to sleep before evening. With this sense of the splendour of our experience and of its awful brevity, gathering all we are into one desperate effort to see and touch, we shall hardly have time to make theories about the things we see and touch. What we have to do is to be for ever curiously testing new opinions and courting new impressions, never acquiescing in a facile orthodoxy of Comte, or of Hegel, or of our own.[7]

Neither viciously nonconformist like the Decadents nor prescriptively orthodox like the mainstream Victorian critics, Pater embraced the need for clearly stated standards yet rejected the proposition that those standards of necessity limit the reader to a rigid, narrow range of interpretive options. Despite his wide-ranging and unconventional opinions on how to approach aesthetic sensation, Pater acknowledged the hierarchical values one expects to find in ethically influenced views of art. In fact, in foregrounding the role of philosophy, he signaled an unwavering sense of the resolute conjunction of some set of moral principles and the highest forms of aesthetic pleasure.

His innovative theoretical approach notwithstanding, Pater's best-known effort to apply his views, his novel *Marius the Epicurean* (1885), fails to fulfill the artistic potential of his convictions. *Marius the Epicurean* affirms Pater's belief in the unity of art and morality by attempting to provide an imaginative context for this view. Unfortunately, the novel's philosophical ambitiousness cannot compensate for its creative weaknesses. The depictions not only of Marius but of all the major characters seem shallow and wooden, and the discourse, following a pattern of pedantic exposition rather of imaginative narration, is a lifeless, mechanical presentation of Pater's aesthetic beliefs. Nonetheless, the novel remains useful for those interested in the artistic context from which *The Picture of Dorian Gray* emerged, for it introduced the significant intellectual issues that Wilde developed in his more accessible and balanced discourse on the relationship between moral values and art.

The most striking difference between *Marius the Epicurean* and *The Picture of Dorian Gray* lies chiefly in their artistic dimensions. Pater's discourse remains firmly under the control of his philosophical concerns; the novel often seems more like an Oxford lecture than a

Victorian novel. Wilde's narrative, on the other hand, though it implicitly acknowledges the impact of his aesthetic views, keeps its author's creative powers in the forefront.

Thus, the narrative of *The Picture of Dorian Gray* endorses the affinity between ethics and aesthetics in a manner that echoes the sentiments of *Marius the Epicurean*. At the same time, the creative achievement of Wilde's work, with its radical but accessible explanation of the association between art and morality, goes far beyond Pater's effort in challenging readers to redefine their own imaginative concepts of this relationship. Specifically, not only does Wilde create interesting characters, but he forms an intriguing premise.

While *The Picture of Dorian Gray* does not prescribe a single answer to the moral questions it raises, it does foreground an ethical program—New Hedonism—that is very different from that governing the lives of most readers. New Hedonism makes a direct claim for the shaping effect of art on individual character, and it articulates the attractiveness of a doctrine of pleasure that absolves individuals from the ordinary responsibilities for their actions. Readers measure the effect of New Hedonism by comparing it to conventional Victorian morality, also found in the narrative, as well as to all the diverse ethical systems, conventional or otherwise, they bring to the text.

The most sustained representation in *The Picture of Dorian Gray* of how this new ethical system challenges the moral positions of both characters and readers appears early on. In chapter 2, Lord Henry introduces the concept of New Hedonism into the discourse during his first conversation with Dorian.

Nothing can cure the soul but the senses, just as nothing can cure the senses but the soul. (20)

Ah! realize your youth while you have it. Don't squander the gold of your days, listening to the tedious, trying to improve the hopeless failure, or giving away your life to the ignorant, the common, and the vulgar. These are the sickly aims, the false ideals, of our age. Live! Live the wonderful life that is in you! Let nothing be lost upon you. Be always searching for new sensations. Be afraid of nothing. . . . [Wilde's ellipsis] A new Hedonism—that is what our century wants. You might be its visible symbol. With your personality there is nothing you could not do. The world belongs to you for a season. (22)

Lord Henry's appeal to Dorian, in language far more direct and imaginative than that of Pater's narrative, unambiguously rejects the call of duty that resonates throughout so much Victorian literature.

Nonetheless, no one in Wilde's novel, least of all Lord Henry, turns his back on the concept of ethical behavior. Despite his frequently extravagant and solipsistic pronouncements, Lord Henry underscores in two important gestures a commitment to his own kind of moral perspective. In his reference to the soul in the first passage quoted above, Lord Henry acknowledges a metaphysical dynamic operating within the human condition while stopping short of suggesting that a set of values could govern behavior. A few pages later, in the second quoted passage, he presents New Hedonism not as a nullification of values but as a hierarchy of standards that contrasts sharply with the world's. Lord Henry's introduction, however, stands as a bare outline of this system. As the narrative unfolds, both he and Dorian provide a far clearer sense of what the ethics of New Hedonism entail. In fact, philosophy and character become so intertwined that understanding someone like Lord Henry depends to a large degree on being able to comprehend the ethical system to which he subscribes.

Such efforts require that the reader show a measure of flexibility, for despite his role as the novel's most vocal exponent of New Hedonism, a great irony informs Lord Henry's character: no matter how extravagant his lexicon of sensualism becomes, he seems to make no move to gratify his appetites. In his case, however, action is not the sole measure of commitment to the system. As readers come to know him, they realize how much satisfaction Lord Henry derives from voyeurism. Through a running commentary on Dorian's life that spans the length of the novel, Lord Henry manages to offer a clear sense of what he believes and of his own detached manner of involvement with

New Hedonism. Early on, for example, he makes clear the privileged position he assigns to any new experience—whether direct or voyeuristic—when he shares with Basil Hallward his reaction to the news of Dorian's engagement to Sibyl Vane.

> If a personality fascinates me, whatever mode of expression that personality selects is absolutely delightful to me. Dorian Gray falls in love with a beautiful girl who acts Juliet, and proposes to marry her. Why not? If he wedded Messalina he would be none the less interesting. You know I am not a champion of marriage. . . . I hope that Dorian Gray will make this girl his wife, passionately adore her for six months, and then suddenly become fascinated by some one else. He would be a wonderful study. (73–74)

Basil protests against this outspoken articulation of New Hedonism by refusing to believe Lord Henry holds views as cynical as his statements suggest: "You don't mean a single word of all that, Harry; you know you don't. If Dorian Gray's life were spoiled, no one would be sorrier than yourself. You are much better than you pretend to be" (74). Lord Henry, however, rebuffs this gesture toward conventional morality and counters it with a highly critical (and some would say insightful) assessment of the pragmatic values that shape human behavior. "The reason we all like to think so well of others is that we are all afraid for ourselves. . . . We praise the banker that we may overdraw our account, and find good qualities in the highwayman in the hope that he may spare our pockets" (74). Embodying more than a jaded cynicism, this statement presents not a rejection of specific human attitudes but rather a dismissal of the hypocrisy that simultaneously holds and yet refuses to acknowledge these attitudes.

Lord Henry's unique ethical positions, however, go beyond the simple negation of popular pieties. In fact, despite his self-proclaimed fascination with artificiality, he bases his mode of conduct on a standard that reflects the influence of the Pre-Raphaelites on his thinking: "Pleasure is the only thing worth having a theory about. . . . But I am afraid that I cannot claim my theory as my own. It belongs to Nature, not to me. Pleasure is Nature's test, her sign of approval. When we are happy we are always good, but when we are good we are not always happy" (77).

Lord Henry's love of paradoxes leads him into some potential imprecision in the final sentence above—the meaning he assigns to the word *good* arguably shifts in midsentence. (It is unclear whether Lord Henry is using *good* to describe a specific action or mode of behavior or to indicate a more general attribute of individual nature). Nonetheless, the association of goodness and pleasure introduces the concept that some forms of action can produce a moral benefit: going back to the thinking first articulated by the Greek philosophers, Lord Henry links goodness and happiness, thus acknowledging the influence of ethical considerations on his view of the world. Of course, Lord Henry's moral values evolve from a subjective consciousness and remain fixed in a marginal position, spurning the conventional markers for right behavior. He tells Dorian as much when he comforts the young man over the death of Sibyl Vane: "Good resolutions are useless attempts to interfere with scientific laws. Their origin is pure vanity. Their result is absolutely *nil*. They give us, now and then, some of those luxurious sterile emotions that have a certain charm for the weak. That is all that can be said for them. They are simply cheques that men draw on a bank where they have no account" (100).

Dorian, like Lord Henry, also subscribes to New Hedonism, but his distinctively different approach to it allows the reader to derive useful insights from observing the contrast. Dorian's attachment to this ethical system grows over the course of the novel, and his active development of its implications—in contrast to Lord Henry's voyeuristic relationship to it—richly illustrates other facets of New Hedonism. Dorian says as much to Lord Henry when he acknowledges his friend's role in sparking the infatuation he develops for Sibyl Vane. "It never would have happened if I had not met you. You filled me with a wild desire to know everything about life" (47–48).

New Hedonism's decree to immerse oneself in unfamiliar sensations is the dominant feature of the love he feels for Sibyl, and it acts as the motivating force guiding his behavior. "Why should I not love her? . . . Night after night I go to see her play. . . . I have seen her in every age and in every costume. Ordinary women never appeal to one's imagination. They are limited to their century. No glamour ever transfigures them. . . . They have their stereotyped smile, and their fashionable manner. They are quite obvious. But an actress! How different an actress is!" (50–51). As the narrative progresses, Dorian becomes more involved in New Hedonism, and its tenets become more obvious to readers. Within this system, gratification emerges as a positive good and constant innovation is the key to sustaining satisfaction, as we see in a passage that records Dorian's efforts to come to grips with the demise of Sibyl Vane.

> When he thought of her, it would be as a wonderful tragic figure sent on to the world's stage to show the supreme reality of Love. A wonderful tragic figure? Tears came to his eyes as he remembered her childlike look and winsome fanciful ways and shy tremulous grace. He brushed them away hastily, and looked again at the picture.
>
> He felt that the time had really come for making his choice. Or had his choice already been made? Yes, life had decided that for him—life, and his own infinite curiosity about life. Eternal youth, infinite passion, pleasures subtle and secret, wild joys and wilder sins—he was to have all these things. The portrait was to bear the burden of his shame: that was all. (105)

This passage marks a crucial point in the narrative: it captures Dorian in the moment of irresolution before he accepts the fact that his private ethics run counter to the public morals of Victorian society. The episode shows, on the one hand, how the transformation of his sorrow over Sibyl's death into a source of satisfaction becomes, for him at least, a positive act coinciding with his new ethical sense. At the same time, the reader sees here that Dorian still feels the need to displace the burden of shame generated by a lingering sense of traditional moral obligation.

Within a short time, however, his ambivalence resolves into a more clearly defined ethical attitude. When Basil Hallward calls on Dorian soon after the death of Sibyl, Dorian's unconventional view of grief clearly shows the increasing influence of New Hedonism on his nature. "It is only shallow people who require years to get rid of an emotion. A man who is master of himself can end a sorrow as easily as he can invent a pleasure. I don't want to be at the mercy of my emotions. I want to use them, to enjoy them, and to dominate them" (108). Under the growing influence of Lord Henry's views, Dorian comes to read Sibyl's suicide from a purely New Hedonistic perspective. "As a rule, people who act lead the most commonplace lives. They are good husbands, or faithful wives, or something tedious. You know what I mean—middle-class virtue, and all that kind of thing. How different Sibyl was! She lived her finest tragedy" (109).

Interpreted from the perspective of conventional morality, this statement belies a fundamental selfishness at the heart of Dorian's argument. On the other hand, the point of view of a New Hedonist reveals an alternative ethical position shaping Dorian's response to Sibyl's death. Like any moralist, he judges Sibyl's behavior according to an accepted set of standards. Such values shock Basil Hallward because they are radically different from his own; nonetheless, the tenets Dorian has now accepted remain consistent as an ethical system.

After the death of Sibyl Vane, Dorian falls increasingly under the influence of the liberating views of this alternative ethical program. A passage in chapter 11 summarizes Dorian's evolving feelings.

Yes: there was to be, as Lord Henry had prophesied, a new Hedonism that was to recreate life, and to save it from the harsh, uncomely puritanism that is having, in our own day, its curious revival. It was to have its service of the intellect, certainly; yet, it was never to accept any theory or system that would involve the sacrifice of any mode of passionate experience. Its aim, indeed, was to be experience itself, and not the fruits of experience, sweet or bitter as they might be. Of the asceticism that deadens the senses, as of the vulgar profligacy that dulls them, it was to know nothing.

But it was to teach man to concentrate himself upon the moments
of a life that is itself but a moment. (130–31)

This stark representation of the aims of New Hedonism presents a
moral view far different from anything expressed in conventional
approaches to ethics. By describing it as a consistent system, however,
Dorian does set up New Hedonism as a viable alternative to traditional values.

Like any outline of a moral structure, Dorian's synopsis of Lord
Henry's explanation of New Hedonism lays out its goals, provides
guidance on achieving them, and establishes a means for judging one's
behavior in relation to the goals. This detailed description of New
Hedonism, however, does not in itself legitimize the alternative ethical
system, and so its function in the discourse is open to debate.
Specifically, the question remains as to whether the system possesses
sufficient depth to provide the necessary ethical support to justify how
Dorian has chosen to live. The discourse of the last two chapters offers
at best an ambiguous answer.

Chapter 19 starts with the proposition that the two leading pro-
ponents of New Hedonism have developed sharply divergent moral
positions. Dorian, in discussing his life with Lord Henry, declares his
intention to follow the conventional path toward reformation. "I have
done too many dreadful things in my life. I am not going to do any
more" (209). Lord Henry, in contrast, remains aloof from the pangs of
conscience produced by ordinary Victorian morality. "Death and vul-
garity are the only two facts in the nineteenth century that one cannot
explain away" (213).

Nonetheless, the disparities between their views are less distinct
than they may initially appear. In fact, even Lord Henry seems to
retain, if not certain traditional scruples, an obvious squeamishness
when invited to consider the most extreme forms of experience that
New Hedonism would sanction. When, for example, Dorian hints at a
personal involvement in a truly violent act—the killing of Basil
Hallward—Lord Henry falls back on what seems to be at best an
equivocal response, and thus he avoids confronting the question of

what limits, if any, he would impose on anyone's efforts to cultivate previously unknown sensations.

> "What would you say, Harry, if I told you that I had murdered Basil?" said the younger man. He watched him intently after he had spoken.
> "I would say, my dear fellow, that you were posing for a character that doesn't suit you. All crime is vulgar, just as all vulgarity is crime. It is not in you, Dorian, to commit a murder. I am sorry if I hurt your vanity by saying so, but I assure you it is true. Crime belongs exclusively to the lower orders. I don't blame them in the smallest degree. I should fancy that crime was to them what art is to us, simply a method of procuring extraordinary sensations."
> (213)

Dorian's question may at first glance seem to affirm his own commitment to the extreme behavior that New Hedonism consistently sanctions. As the conversation continues, however, Dorian seems to reconsider his commitment, and he refuses to indulge Lord Henry's efforts to avoid consideration of the conventional moral consequences of behavior. Instead, he turns their discussion to a reflection on the metaphysical implications of all human action. "The soul is a terrible reality. It can be bought, and sold, and bartered away. It can be poisoned, or made perfect. There is a soul in each one of us. I know it" (215).

Lord Henry, on the other hand, continues to resist confronting the full implications of New Hedonism, and his responses blithely sidestep the serious issues that Dorian raises. Instead of engaging Dorian's doubts, as he has at several points earlier in the narrative, Lord Henry completely avoids thinking about consequences and responsibility by denying the existence of the soul as the metaphysical force that would validate such concerns: "The things one feels absolutely certain about are never true" (215). Previously, of course, he had shown no such hesitation in considering metaphysical matters, as when he referred to the soul as part of an argument demonstrating the efficacy of New Hedonism: "Nothing can cure the soul but the senses, just as nothing can cure the senses but the soul" (20). In his apparent inconsistency, his unwillingness to confront Dorian's most extreme example of living the tenets of New Hedonism—murder as a new experience—Lord Henry shows at the very least an imperfect acceptance of the system he has articulated so forcefully on earlier occasions.

Nevertheless, Lord Henry does retain a basic fidelity, however imperfect, to New Hedonism. Earlier in chapter 19, when told of Dorian's decision not to seduce Hetty Merton, Lord Henry dismisses his friend's halting efforts to re-embrace conventional morality through reformation as nothing more than an attempt to acquire a previously unknown experience. "I should think the novelty of the emotion must have given you a thrill of real pleasure" (210).

Lord Henry's remarks show that his commitment to New Hedonism remains so strong that he can give no real credence to the idea of Dorian returning to the more restrictive regime of conventional Victorian principles. Lord Henry, in fact, goes beyond simply rationalizing Dorian's apparently minor deviations from the values of New Hedonism. He singles out his friend's life as an ideal representation of how an individual lives in accordance with this alternative ethical system.

> I wish I could change places with you, Dorian. The world has cried out against us both, but it has always worshipped you. It always will worship you. You are the type of what the age is searching for, and what it is afraid it has found. I am so glad that you have never done anything, never carved a statue, or painted a picture, or produced anything outside of yourself! Life has been your art. You have set yourself to music. Your days are your sonnets. (217)

Dorian's unwillingness to take comfort in such compliments, however, attests to his growing ambivalence toward the spiritual satisfaction New Hedonism can provide, and readers must now ponder how to assess most effectively the ethical implications of his vacillating behavior. Underscoring this conflict are the parallels in the final chapter with the scene at the close of chapter 7 after Dorian's confrontation with Sibyl Vane but before he has learned of her death. In the earlier episode, Dorian discovers the first slight change that has insinuated itself into his picture, and he resolves—only temporarily, as it turns out—to reform his life.

> Yet it was watching him, with its beautiful marred face and its cruel smile. Its bright hair gleamed in the early sunlight. Its blue eyes met his own. A sense of infinite pity, not for himself, but for the painted image of himself, came over him. It had altered already, and would alter more. Its gold would wither into grey. Its red and white roses would die. For every sin that he committed, a stain would fleck and wreck its fairness. But he would not sin. The picture, changed or unchanged would be to him the visible emblem of conscience. He would resist temptation. (91–92)

In the closing pages of chapter 20, Dorian once again turns hopefully to the picture, this time to assess the effect on it of his resisting the temptation to seduce Hetty Merton. The ongoing corruption that it reveals instead underscores for Dorian and for the reader the possibility that Lord Henry's comments about the motivations for Dorian's actions may have been more accurate than the younger man had wished to admit. "A cry of pain and indignation broke from him. He could see no change, save that in the eyes there was a look of cunning, and in the mouth the curved wrinkle of the hypocrite" (221). Within moments of this discovery, in apparent reaction to the painting's continuing degeneration, Dorian seizes the same knife he had used to murder Basil Hallward and stabs the picture, thus killing himself.

Despite the obvious closure this gesture imposes on the action of the novel, Dorian's final deed does little to dispel the ambiguity that has surrounded the discourse's representation of ethical values. Did New Hedonism fail Dorian, or did he fail to make a sufficient commitment to its tenets? His attack on the painting itself resolves Dorian's fate, but it also raises issues related to how our judgment of ethical principles conditions our broad interpretations of the action in *The Picture of Dorian Gray*.

This question cannot be definitively answered by simply reexamining the narrative, for too many variables intervene and make valid a range of diverse interpretations. Nevertheless, any number of readers have offered definitive, albeit very different interpretations based on ethical positions ranging from harsh condemnation to unqualified approval of Dorian's behavior.[8] Although each reading contributes illuminating perspectives on Dorian's nature and on the disposition of the narrative discourse, none of them can offer more than a partial resolution of the ethical issues raised by the novel.

We see once again the benefits of the multiple-interpretations approach outlined in chapter 4. The scope of valid alternative analyses of *The Picture of Dorian Gray* requires a method for determining meaning that draws directly on the ethical perspective of the individual reader while acknowledging the range of alternative views that contribute to a full sense of the ethical-aesthetic meaning of the work.[9] This feature of the discourse, however, has even broader implications.

In fact, the shifts in the narrative discourse between ethical positions illustrate the importance of an interpretive model constructed along the lines I have suggested in previous chapters. The solipsism of New Hedonism frankly appeals to the ego of every reader, but pressure to conform to social mores, which recurs throughout the narrative, is also familiar to us all. As we confront the ambiguities of the ethics of New Hedonism, we face, more directly than in most acts of interpretation, the impact on our aesthetic sense of our own moral values. Thus, assessing *The Picture of Dorian Gray* gives us the self-reflexive opportunity to increase our awareness of the principles that shape our interpretive assumptions.

The novel is so much more than a simple philosophical exercise: it enables us to indulge a range of alternative ethical responses to the central issues it raises without incurring the consequences such behavior would provoke in reality. Thus, *The Picture of Dorian Gray*—like *Oedipus Rex*, *King Lear*, and *Paradise Lost*—builds on our own ethical values. More to the point, however, it illuminates these values and those of alternative ethical systems within the security of an artistic milieu, without a sense of guilt or responsibility for what occurs.

In consequence, *The Picture of Dorian Gray* does not—and should not—bring us to a new ethical position or reinforce our old one. Rather, through the actions of its characters, it impresses on us a sense of the wide-ranging aesthetic force that ethics exerts on a work of art. Furthermore, Wilde's novel gives us the opportunity to enhance our awareness of aesthetic and ethical values by extending our sense of the possibilities for interpretation beyond those outlined by more familiar approaches.

6

The Resonance of Sensuality

The only way to get rid of a temptation is to yield to it.
The Picture of Dorian Gray

Chapters 4 and 5 highlighted the ways in which a range of meanings influence a reader's analysis of *The Picture of Dorian Gray*. In this chapter, I explore how varied and often overlapping views of the narrative structure influence each reader's interpretation of *The Picture of Dorian Gray*—specifically, by examining how the attitudes toward sensuality held by the characters, the readers, and the author produce a range of unique, often unconventional readings.

Internal and external elements shape individual responses to *The Picture of Dorian Gray* in three stages: they combine to influence the interpretive expectations readers bring to the novel; this combined influence plays itself out in the narrative by supporting a range of equally valid responses to the novel; and finally, each reader's full perception of this interaction enhances the aesthetic pleasure he or she derives from the work.

This process of identifying and balancing the effects of internal and external elements may seem to lead directly to predictable, if sometimes rather involved explanations of meaning within the work. When, for example, the narrative draws attention to the characters' differing views of social conditions and to their perceptions of class differences, the reader's interpretive choice of accepting the opinions of either one character or another seems quite clear—for instance, Dorian's attitude or Lord Henry's contrasting attitude toward charity work in the East End (15); Lord Henry's and Basil Hallward's different responses to Dorian's engagement to Sibyl Vane (73–75); and the different perspectives of Sibyl and her brother as they observe the crowd in Hyde Park (68–69). In each instance, the narrative asks readers to consider the reactions of Wilde's characters to selected social disparities, to balance these responses against their own initial reactions, and to come to an interpretation of each scene. The narrative supports the possibility of accepting any of a variety of views based on the reader's own perceptions of class. Nonetheless, for most readers, the different options remain sharp and distinct.

This wide choice of possible meanings can in fact produce an abundance of interpretive difficulties. Obviously, when alternative meanings are possible, the problem of reconciling sharply different views into a unified and coherent response becomes more pronounced. Relying on abstract cultural values, like individual goodness, does not always provide the reader with clear interpretive options and in fact can lead to contradictory impressions, which in turn introduce a range of conflicting choices that the reader can neither easily harmonize nor readily ignore.

The ethical systems outlined in chapter 5, for example, do not always provide clear guidelines for addressing specific aspects of sensuality, particularly as it appears in *The Picture of Dorian Gray*. As a result, unlike other interpretive problems that the reader can clarify by referring to precisely defined social standards, the tension created in certain passages by a clash between personal values and the apparent direction of the narrative sometimes heightens the reader's uneasiness and diminishes his or her tolerance for alternative responses. Some readers will try to relieve this tension by ignoring apparent options and imposing a single response that suppresses alternative interpretations in favor of a dominant view.[1]

This inclination seems nowhere more apparent than in the reactions of some critics to the numerous representations of hedonism that fill the narrative of *The Picture of Dorian Gray*. I have noted the range of these responses already and so will not elaborate on them again except to characterize them here as, in the main, exculpatory, condemnatory, or celebratory. Each type of critic necessarily distorts or ignores selected portions of the novel in order to frame an argument that successfully supports his or her polemical position. That many critics often reductively conflate the issue of sensuality to encompass only eroticism—or even more reductively, homoeroticism—confirms my point.

The more extreme positions of such critics can be easily dismissed; nevertheless, the reader cannot ignore the need to address the issue of sensuality coherently and to resolve the apparent interpretive contradictions arising from alternative points of views. Early in the narrative, for example, Lord Henry Wotton offers the following analysis of Dorian Gray's inner nature. His observations sharply focus attention on the emotional stress felt by characters experiencing the conflicting power of sexual desire and puritanical repression. "You, Mr. Gray, you yourself, with your rose-red youth and your rose-white boyhood, you have had passions that have made you afraid, thoughts that have filled you with terror, day-dreams and sleeping dreams whose mere memory might stain your cheek with shame" (18). At first glance, it seems fairly apparent that Lord Henry is making a direct attempt to lead Dorian Gray to acknowledge the depth of his own sensuality. A closer look at the structure that frames Lord Henry's remarks, however, invites the reader to consider a range of possible responses.

The formal organization of Lord Henry's statement places his views in a complex psychological and social context and highlights our awareness of the multiple meanings that can be found in his words: although he refers to feelings common to every young man, he magnifies the impact of his remarks by using language that invokes powerful cultural metaphors. The patronizing formality of "Mr. Gray," for example, immediately reminds the modern reader of the hierarchical social conventions that set the late-Victorian period apart from our own. As noted in chapter 4, the allegorical floral imagery that follows—"your rose-red youth and your rose-white boyhood"—clearly emphasizes the fragile, temporary quality of Dorian's physical beauty and suggests imaginative associations with fantastic characters and unreal situations through its evocation of the fairy-tale figures Snow White and Rose Red. Finally, the psychologically charged arrangement of references to private imaginative musings and to personal guilt ("thoughts," "day-dreams," "stain," "shame") invites the reader to form implicit associations between hidden sensuality and disgraceful desires. All of these reflections, of course, come to us through the refined sensibilities of Lord Henry's New Hedonism.

Lord Henry's words underscore the argumentative skill of a practiced debater, enhanced by the rhetoric of insinuation. They relentlessly call into question the predictable moral conclusions that we would conventionally draw. The rich multiplicity of Lord Henry's rhetoric invites the reader to develop a sophisticated, multifaceted comprehension of sensuality similar to the voluptuous awareness Lord Henry encourages Dorian to cultivate.

Because of its cultural context, however, the appeal made here to the reader takes on even greater significance. Through Lord Henry's discourse, Wilde carefully invokes the sexual associations imbedded deeply within the complex social vocabulary of the Victorian age. The narrative, while not denying the raw power of physical desire, is keenly attentive to the societal forces that shape the responses to sexual issues of both Dorian and the readers. By raising those issues indirectly, *The Picture of Dorian Gray* acknowledges the complexity of these feelings and, through Lord Henry, implicitly encourages an openness to multiple perspectives in assessing them.[2]

As argued in chapter 4, no single point of view has proved sufficient to describe completely the narrative lines that develop in *The Picture of Dorian Gray*, so it comes as no surprise when Lord Henry shows a prodigious talent for wringing a range of meanings from even the most pedestrian of ideas. This talent is more than a characterizing feature of his nature; it functions as an interpretive model that the narrative invites readers to follow. Lord Henry's rhetoric teases us with suggestions of stereotypical Victorian thinking, but in the end his remarks take late-nineteenth-century clichés to extremes that give them new life: commonplace sayings become rich discourses on the alternatives ways of perceiving Victorian society.

Many readings of *The Picture of Dorian Gray*, however, have shown little sensitivity to the interpretive diversity fostered by the narrative and instead take a single, dominant approach. Of course, Wilde's novel readily supports interpretations that offer highly specific and opinionated commentaries on the nineteenth-century world Dorian inhabits. In fact, a central point of my own analysis is that we can accept these and many other highly directive approaches. At the same time, however, when any analysis implicitly or explicitly presents itself as the single best approach, it inevitably succumbs to the reductive impulse to claim that the novel can be best appreciated only from its perspective. Wilde's narrative discourse systematically undercuts such a position.

I must state in fairness that very few critics of *The Picture of Dorian Gray* claim that their views should have primacy over all others. At the same time, many follow methodologies that take no notice of other positions and end up presenting their views as if there were no viable alternatives. Such exclusion, whatever its intention, in effect denies the efficacy of other readings while privileging the one presented.

As noted in chapter 3, ample evidence of the shortsightedness of prescriptive criticism can be found in some of the newspaper reviews of the *Lippincott's* novella version of *The Picture of Dorian Gray*.[3] Although Victorian journalists did not address sexual issues directly, the tone of their newspaper columns left readers in little doubt that their objections to *The Picture of Dorian Gray* centered on the novel's overt sensuality. Over the last 100 years, judgments of Wilde's depiction of sensuality have shifted markedly, moving from disapproval through ambivalence toward outright admiration. Unfortunately, despite this welcome shift away from ill-considered condemnation, a number of contemporary critics retain the old compulsion to make rudimentary yet sweeping moral judgments. In fact, two of the best-known studies of Wilde, written during the 1970s, stop short of praising Dorian's asocial behavior but take up critical positions as simplistic as those held by Wilde's contemporaries.

Christopher Nassaar, in stark Manichaean terms, interprets *The Picture of Dorian Gray* as a Faustian struggle between good and evil for Dorian's soul.[4] Nassaar shows an accurate sense of the breadth of the novel by dwelling on the effect of general conditions in forming Dorian's character. The final pages of his long chapter devoted to *The Picture of Dorian Gray*, however, in assessing representations of sexuality, shift the argument to a far narrower concern. Nassaar's fairly reductive view is that the novel depicts sensual desire as a destructive force—specifically, because of its homosexual manifestation. Surprisingly, Nassaar does not seem to take heterosexual drives into consideration; his examination of Dorian's relationship with Sibyl Vane, for example, concentrates exclusively on the aesthetic attraction he feels. Thus, sexual preference as depicted in the novel becomes for Nassaar not simply a neutral element of individual nature but a gauge of goodness or depravity, with homosexual inclinations providing evidence of a fatal flaw in character.[5]

Philip Cohen, author of the other prominent thematic study from this period, initially seems less prescriptive in his characterizations of sensuality in *The Picture of Dorian Gray*.[6] Unfortunately, his assessment of the role of eroticism in the narrative extends no further than regretting that "the novel does not clearly and consistently maintain a single moral position." Cohen goes on to emphasize his own need for certitude by characterizing this shifting condition in *The Picture of Dorian Gray* as a reflection of Wilde's own "moral ambivalence [revealed] through his careless, naive use of the self-conscious narrator."[7] Finally, a disappointing tendency toward oversimplification emerges as his interpretation of Wilde's novel develops. Cohen abandons any tolerance for complexity and instead advocates a simplistic, puritanical conception of morality, criticizing Wilde whenever the narrative seems to stray from that standard.

A few contemporaries of Nassaar and Cohen offered alternative approaches. They presented dispassionate views of the sensuality of the novel's homoeroticism, simply identifying it as a central feature of the novel without taking the matter further. However, their refusal to come to grips with the moral implications of sensuality often produces deadly dull responses.

Rupert Croft-Cooke, for example, takes this nominally objective approach to the point of absurdity by restricting his analysis to making analogies between the central characters in *The Picture of Dorian Gray* and "their homosexual counterparts in real life."[8] Identifying homoerotic elements in the novel may, with elaboration, be a useful contribution to a broader reading of the work, but interpretations that do little more than establish biographical associations based on sexual preference are too limited and come across as a kind of retrospective "outing." Moreover, the validity of specific identifications has come into question when other critics, writing with similar assurance, have named different men as the models for the main characters.[9]

More recently, scholars pursuing questions of homosexual allusions in *The Picture of Dorian Gray* have taken far more polemical positions. Just as certain Victorian writers tried to label Wilde as a man without morals and to dismiss his novel as a celebration of scandalous immorality, now his defenders seek—anachronistically, in my view—to ennoble him as a spokesperson for gay activism and his novel as a manifesto for alternative living.[10] Over the past two decades, a number of interpretations have offered sympathetic readings of *The Picture of Dorian Gray* as a homosexual treatise and of Wilde as a vigorous advocate of a homosexual lifestyle.[11] Though markedly different in content from the studies of scholars like Philip Cohen and Christopher Nassaar, these critics have proven similarly unwilling to accept alternative interpretations of the aesthetic effect of the novel's sensuality. Readers of both types tend to place Wilde outside society and to see him as an iconoclast.

Even a critic extremely sensitive to the nuances of social context can fall into narrowly defining the options found in Wilde's narrative. Regenia Gagnier, for example, begins her sophisticated assessment of *The Picture of Dorian Gray* by exploring how its discourse sustains a range of readings of its representation of sensuality. She perceptively contrasts the likely interpretations of different readers: "Members of the homosexual community could read *Dorian Gray* sympathetically, for characters like Hallward were the staple of their literature. . . . On the other hand, because of the story's obliqueness regarding Dorian's sins and, especially, its entirely moralistic conclusions, journalists could only hint at their suspicions concerning Wilde."[12]

In these remarks, Gagnier acknowledges several simultaneous ways to respond to *The Picture of Dorian Gray*, providing a useful balance to alternative readings, but she continues to assume that the reader must make exclusive choices when interpreting the novel. That is, the reader must put Wilde among either the gays or the straights, seeing him, by implication, as either at the center of moral Victorian society or completely outside its jurisdiction. These alternatives still do not capture the complexity of the novel. Instead, because she interprets biographical details a certain way, Gagnier holds that an interpretation of the sensuality in *The Picture of Dorian Gray* that most closely parallels Wilde's own attitudes should take precedence over all others.

In fact, as a number of astute cultural critics have already shown, for most of his life Oscar Wilde's behavior placed him neither outside nor at the center of late-nineteenth-century English society.[13] Instead, at least until the notorious Queensberry trials of 1895 that culminated in Wilde's imprisonment for two years on charges of immoral behavior, he cultivated his pose as a Dandy, inhabiting an intentionally ambiguous position near the margins but always within the bounds of Victorian society. This same duality characterizes the organization of *The Picture of Dorian Gray*.[14]

Moreover, the clearest illustration of the diverse sensuality that defines both the principal characters and the direction of the discourse is found in this hybrid image of the Dandy that Wilde created in his fiction. The Dandy was a figure with a long history and dominated popular culture throughout the nineteenth century; nevertheless, Wilde managed to depict his Dandy characters in a highly sophisticated and a very specialized manner.[15] Unlike some of their predecessors, Wilde's Dandies emerge as characters who thrive on a mutually beneficial relationship with their society.

The Dandies of *The Picture of Dorian Gray*—most notably Dorian himself and Lord Henry Wotton—set themselves apart by straining against conventional restrictions, but they always remain careful never to go so far as to isolate themselves from those around them. These Dandies critique but never directly oppose the society they inhabit: through their words and actions, they seek to arouse the interest of the general public, but they also try to prevent public disapproval from reaching the point that would lead to their ostracism.[16] Most significantly, Wilde's Dandies are not motivated only by gross physical drives. Rather, they are complete sensualists, open to any experience that touches their senses.

This expanded image of the Dandy supports a number of approaches to *The Picture of Dorian Gray* and counters inclinations toward reductive readings, such as those by critics who see the novel as either a celebration or a condemnation of a particular form of sexuality. The novel's representation of the Dandy's point of view underscores Wilde's emphatically pluralistic response to social values.

The most immediate example of the narrative's presentation of sensuality in multiple forms, and the one that calls into question all the simplistic interpretations of sensuality cited above, comes early on in Basil Hallward's admission to Lord Henry of the hold Dorian Gray has over him. Basil's description of his initial meeting with Dorian and his summaries of every subsequent encounter consistently emphasize the young man's beauty. At the same time, Basil's account of his response goes deeper than a description of mere physical attraction and touches on a more profound, less easily categorized imaginative power that Dorian's nature exerts: "I turned half-way round, and saw Dorian Gray for the first time. When our eyes met, I felt that I was growing pale. A curious sensation of terror came over me. I knew that I had come face to face with some one whose mere personality was so fascinating that, if I allowed it to do so, it would absorb my whole nature, my whole soul, my very art itself" (6).

Despite the apparent explicitness of this and similar remarks, the reader needs to be very careful in assessing the attitude Basil describes, for Wilde's narrative rigorously resists any easy classification of complex feelings. In every instance, Basil frankly admires Dorian's beauty, and certainly an aura of homoeroticism seems to inform all their exchanges. On closer scrutiny, however, his admiration seems always to be merely a preliminary sensation. Events clearly show that Basil draws on Dorian for a far more complex set of responses, extending well beyond the gratification of physical desire: "Dorian Gray is to me simply a motive in art. You might see nothing in him. I see everything in him. He is never more present in my work than when no image of him is there. He is a suggestion, as I have said, of a new manner. I find him in the curves of certain lines, in the loveliness and subtleties of certain colours" (11).

This excitement that Dorian arouses certainly grows out of Basil's sensual appetites, but it more specifically reflects an artist's aesthetic concerns, which ultimately turn attention away from the model and toward the creation: "Every portrait that is painted with feeling is a portrait of the artist, not of the sitter. The sitter is merely the accident, the occasion. It is not he who is revealed by the painter; it is rather the painter who, on the coloured canvas, reveals himself. The reason I will not exhibit this picture is that I am afraid that I have shown in it the secret of my own soul" (5). If the reader sees Dorian as the representation of the sensual forces in the novel—and indeed that seems precisely what all the critics cited here have done—then clearly our concept of sensuality must encompass the absolute scope of his appeal. This reading, of necessity, would include his full aesthetic impact, not simply focusing on sexual reverberations.

By the same token, it would be a mistake simply to see Basil's attitude toward Dorian as the dispassionate view of an artist toward a particularly useful model. As the events of chapters 12 and 13 make clear, Basil's efforts to move Dorian toward reform obviously demonstrate a kind of love. The love Basil expresses, however, is inherently idealistic, and characterizing it as mere physical desire trivializes a very powerful and complex emotion: "Pray, Dorian, pray. . . . The prayer of your pride has been answered. The prayer of your repentance will be answered also. I worshipped you too much. I am punished for it. Your worshipped yourself too much. We are both punished" (157–58).

Obviously, Basil's awkward expression, combining piety and infatuation, reflects his own imperfect comprehension of the diverse feelings that make up his attitude toward Dorian. Nonetheless, the range of these views lends equal support to a number of possible interpretations of the nature of their relationship. Assuredly, that variety cannot be accommodated by favoring one or another aspect of a very complex association. Consequently, critics who cite Basil's attitude toward Dorian to support the view that *The Picture of Dorian Gray* articulates a defense of homosexuality, or who use it to prove that the novel illustrates the unfortunate consequences of attempts to flout conventional morality, are led into the trap of reductivism. Elements of *The Picture of Dorian Gray* can certainly be used to support either view, but these arguments cannot legitimately be made in ways that suppress other manifestations of sensuality.

Furthermore, in examining the different possible responses to Dorian's relations with Basil, the reader becomes more aware of the various ways in which the natures of other characters in the novel can be interpreted. This realization, in turn, gives us a better idea of how to balance the novel's conflicting depictions of sensuality and how to elaborate on our initial impressions.

The narrative seems to present Sibyl Vane, for example, as much more than simply a female counterpart to Basil Hallward. Admittedly, her love of Dorian appears to dominate her just as Basil's affection for the young man rules him. Nonetheless, the relationship itself is much more complex. In contrast to his aloof disregard for Basil's feelings, Dorian reciprocates Sibyl's love with, initially at least, an equal or greater intensity: "Why should I not love her? Harry, I do love her. She is everything to me in life. Night after night I go to see her play. . . . I have seen her in every age and in every costume. Ordinary women never appeal to one's imagination. They are limited to their century. . . . But an actress! How different an actress is! Harry! why didn't you tell me that the only thing worth loving is an actress?" (50–51).

In this passage, Dorian in fact describes very nearly the same sense of imaginative pleasure to which Basil refers in outlining his fascination with Dorian. For readers pursuing a single-track approach to sensuality, Dorian's devotion signals a shift from the homosexual emphasis of the earlier chapters (underscored not only by Basil's devotion to Dorian but by Dorian's petulant, girlish willfulness) to a heterosexual orientation. As the reader progresses through the novel, however, it becomes apparent that emphasizing gender distinctions is as reductive a way to assess the attraction between Dorian and Sibyl as it is in judging the relationship between Dorian and Basil.

Like Basil's regard for his model, Dorian's devotion to Sibyl Vane reflects a broad spectrum of desires. Dorian, like Basil, feels caught up by the newness of every sensation and intoxicated by every experience. Sibyl has touched Dorian in a way that is preeminently sensual without necessarily being sexual. (Indeed, his volatile reaction to Lord Henry's probing questions about the degree of physical intimacy in his relationship with her reveals an almost morbid puritanism: "Harry! Sibyl Vane is sacred" [51]).

Paradoxically, however, Dorian has a much more superficial sense of Sibyl than Basil has of him. The dramatic roles that Sibyl assumes on stage, rather than her own nature, are what attract Dorian. He ingenuously says as much when in response to Lord Henry's question "When is she Sibyl Vane?" he replies, "Never" (54). Sibyl has stirred Dorian's imagination in much the same way Dorian has affected Basil's aesthetic sense, but unlike Basil, Dorian has no sense of the humanity behind the stimulus.

Basil himself does much to impress on the reader's consciousness these parallel aesthetic effects. After learning of Dorian's engagement to Sibyl, he defends the act from Lord Henry's cynicism: "Don't pay any attention to him, Dorian. . . . I understand what you mean, and I believe in this girl. Any one you love must be marvellous, and any girl that has the effect you describe must be fine and noble" (81). Although Basil does not single out aesthetics as the central feature of Dorian's affection, his words do underscore the importance of the transforming effect on the imagination of certain types of affection. Basil's remarks, in fact, highlight Sibyl's power to create an imaginative effect rather than physical desire. His observations direct readers toward abundance and away from exclusiveness, expanding our notions of sensuality and sensory gratification and unconsciously laying the groundwork for Dorian's final rejection of Sibyl.

Of course, for readers attentive to the complex portrayal of sensual experience in *The Picture of Dorian Gray*, the termination of Dorian's engagement to Sibyl is the inevitable consequence of how the actress perceives the world. Like the critics with narrow views on sensuality cited earlier, Sibyl sees love as an unambiguous and monolithic condition, overpowering all else and focusing her imagination on a single feature. "Dorian . . . before I knew you, acting was the one reality of my life. It was only in the theatre that I lived. I thought that it was all true. . . . You taught me what reality really is. . . . You brought me something higher, something of which all art is but a reflection. You had made me understand what love really is" (85–86).

Dorian, unfortunately, responds with equal force. He finds that the very single-mindedness of Sibyl's love, the complete concentration of her imagination on it, deadens his feeling of attraction for her: "You have killed my love. You used to stir my imagination. Now you don't even stir my curiosity. You simply produce no effect. I loved you because you were marvellous, because you had genius and intellect, because you realized the dreams of great poets and gave shape and substance to the shadows of art. You have thrown it all away. You are shallow and stupid" (86–87).

Although the force of this dismissal cannot be denied, a simplistic reading of his blunt declaration should be avoided. As in assessing Basil's feelings, viewing Dorian's gesture merely in terms of glutted desire, distracted sexual urges, or transient romantic inclinations reduces a series of complex attitudes to the level of cliché. In fact, to get a full sense of the imaginative potential of this portion of the narrative, the reader must interpret Dorian's behavior along the same lines as those applied to assessments of Basil's actions earlier.

In both instances, appreciation of the full range of human sensuality prohibits the imposition of a single dominant interpretation of the character's actions. Like Basil's feelings for him, Dorian arguably finds satisfaction in a range of the physical and imaginative elements that characterize Sibyl's nature: beauty, sexuality, artistic power, grace, expressiveness, openness. In both characters, the reader must be prepared to allow these complex and contradictory feelings to coexist.

Dorian's tangled relations with Sibyl expand the emotional scope of the novel and introduce another element into our response to sensuality in *The Picture of Dorian Gray*. Specifically, Sibyl's suicide and Dorian's responsibility for triggering it raise new moral questions (similar to those examined in detail in chapter 5) for the reader. In two crucial passages, the discourse presents New Hedonism's unabashed appetite for sensory pleasure. In the passage above, Dorian responds to

Sibyl's failure to provide that gratification with the harsh language of dismissal (86–87). With equal bluntness, the narrative depicts the chilling consequences of this attitude in Lord Henry's fatalistic argument (100–103) that Dorian should not allow Sibyl's death to affect him. Lord Henry's final remarks graphically illustrate the place of sensuality and gratification in the life of a New Hedonist:

> [Sibyl] has played her last part. But you must think of that lonely death in the tawdry dressing-room simply as a strange lurid fragment from some Jacobean tragedy, as a wonderful scene from Webster, or Ford, or Cyril Tourneur. The girl never really lived, and so she has never really died. To you at least she was always a dream, a phantom that flitted through Shakespeare's plays and left them lovelier for its presence, a reed through which Shakespeare's music sounded richer and more full of joy. The moment she touched actual life, she marred it, and it marred her, and so she passed away. Mourn for Ophelia, if you like. Put ashes on your head because Cordelia was strangled. Cry out against Heaven because the daughter of Brabantio died. But don't waste your tears over Sibyl Vane. She was less real than they are. (103)

The reader cannot ignore the brutality of this speech, and indeed, the narrative implicitly invites us to make a moral judgment of Lord Henry. At the same time, the shifting points of view that have already appeared in the discourse serve as a warning against forming hasty generalizations.

As *The Picture of Dorian Gray* unfolds, the possible range of responses expands as the reader develops a clear sense of Dorian's broad appetite for different experiences. The narrative reflects this diversity and suggests with growing force that each reading must take the alternative possibilities for interpretation into account. Chapter 11, for example, is suffused with elaborate descriptions of Dorian's fascination with various sensations, and it becomes evident that the wide-ranging hedonism that dominates his consciousness goes far beyond mere eroticism. It also becomes obvious to the careful reader that such diverse experiences necessarily lend themselves to different interpretations based on different ethical responses.

The pleasures cataloged in chapter 11 subtly but insistently challenge conventional expectations about Dorian's pursuit of gratification. The catalog includes the predictable debaucheries in the poor sections of London as well as the licentiousness among men and women of Dorian's own class. But the chapter also records the more esoteric aesthetic pleasures: Dorian's interest in Roman Catholic liturgy, his joy as a collector in artifacts that appeal to a range of senses (perfumes, music, jewels, embroideries), and his intellectual gratification as a student of literature.

In mixing sensations both licit and illicit (at least as conventionally defined), the discourse overturns the easy, stereotypical contrasts of good versus evil. Unlike Milton's Satan, whose pleasure depends completely on ethical standards (if what he does is not evil, there is no satisfaction in it for him), Dorian's gratification oscillates between physical and metaphysical concerns. He does not predictably enjoy an experience or not because it is good or evil according to conventional standards. Rather, his reactions hinge on how an experience does or does not provide him with pleasure.

Of course, each reader's personal views of sensuality cannot fail to shape his or her interpretation. Dorian's obsessive pursuit of pleasure, for example, could lead someone committed to a conventional interpretation of the novel to characterize his behavior as that of a sociopath, a type whose amorality defines him as clearly as would undisputed confirmation of his goodness or evil. Indeed, at times the narrative's stark depiction of Dorian's calculated pursuit of self-gratification seems to encourage just such a view: "But he never fell into the error of arresting his intellectual development by any formal acceptance of creed or system, or of mistaking, for a house in which to live, an inn that is but suitable for the sojourn of a night, or for a few hours of a night in which there are no stars and the moon is in travail" (133). At the same time, a reader committed to a set of values as different as New Hedonism would make a markedly different assessment of his behavior, seeing it as entirely in keeping with the qualities esteemed by that system.

As noted earlier, however, a variety of ethical systems significantly influence how the reader perceives action in the narrative, and there is no need to assume that these systems all conform to conventional expectations about sensuality. In fact, as is apparent from this chapter's examination of several characters, the discourse takes pains to subvert such easy generalizations. Nonetheless, the narrative consistently affirms the relationship between some set of values and Dorian's consciousness by keeping descriptions of the portrait and of Dorian's fear of public exposure solidly before the reader:

> He hated to be separated from the picture that was such a part of his life, and was also afraid that during his absence some one might gain access to the room, in spite of the elaborate bars that he had cause to be placed upon the door.
>
> What if it should be stolen? The mere thought made him cold with horror. Surely the world would know his secret then. Perhaps the world already knew. (141)

Thus, even at the end of the section that has devoted so much space to the classification of sensual response, the reader still cannot easily or definitively categorize Dorian's behavior.

The subsequent chapters make such judgments even more problematic. Early in the novel, Dorian's apparent contribution to Sibyl Vane's decision to commit suicide insistently draws attention to ethical issues. At the same time, the narrative comes to no clear-cut conclusion on the matter but rather calls on each reader to determine his degree of complicity. His murder of Basil Hallward, however, seems to dispel any moral ambivalence a reader may still have had in assessing Dorian's sensuality. With that act, Dorian undeniably—at least in the eyes of most readers—crosses the line between selfish pursuit of personal gratification and arrogant disregard for all others. Indeed, the description of his awakening on the morning after the killing seems to confirm such a view, providing as it does a chilling account of his lack of remorse for his crime. "Dorian was sleeping quite peacefully. . . . He looked like a boy who had been tired out with play, or study . . . and as he opened his eyes a faint smile passed across his lips, as though he had been lost in some delightful dream. Yet he had not dreamed at all. His night had been untroubled by any images of pleasure or of pain" (162).

Almost immediately, however, the narrative checks the inevitable condemnations that would flow out of such linear thinking. While the novel does not deny Dorian's seemingly heartless feelings, within a few pages it questions whether this image of the uncaring sensualist fully represents his character. Specifically, the reader sees Dorian in an unexpectedly vulnerable position, taking great pains to shield the feelings of Alan Campbell even while blackmailing him into disposing of Basil's body (169–72). The narrative successively emphasizes paradoxical, if not conflicting views of Dorian's character and leaves to the reader the task of reconciling them. Even in these extremes, however, neither the image of the determined blackmailer nor that of the stricken friend completely describes Dorian's nature. Thus, readers may understandably have difficulty forming their responses to his unbridled sensuality from a single moral perspective, no matter how flexible.

Further evidence of Dorian's inconsistent ethical position in relation to his appetite for sensory gratification only magnifies the task of reconciliation. For example, just a few pages after the death of James Vane interrupts his efforts to lead the Duchess of Monmouth into adultery, Dorian apparently reverses his priorities and (as discussed already in chapter 5) tells Lord Henry of his intention to change by resisting the temptation to seduce a young country girl, Hetty Merton. As readers begin to contemplate Dorian's final reformation, Lord Henry steps in to offer another possibility. As always, he remains skeptical of appearances and reluctant to abandon his own opinions, and so he glosses the incident with a cynicism that seems truly to shock Dorian.

> "We were to have gone away together this morning at dawn. Suddenly I determined to leave her as flower-like as I had found her."
>
> "I should think the novelty of the emotion must have given you a thrill of real pleasure, Dorian," interrupted Lord Henry.

"But I can finish your idyll for you. You gave her good advice, and broke her heart. That was the beginning of your reformation."

"Harry, you are horrible! You mustn't say these dreadful things." (210)

Just as Dorian, the committed New Hedonist, remains open to a range of sensual pleasures, so also must the committed reader remain open to a range of possible responses to the narrative. Further, just as the committed New Hedonist would not hear of rationing pleasures or sampling them one at a time, so also must the committed reader acknowledge the variety of meanings offered by the narrative. The New Hedonist does not go about seeking the best pleasure while ignoring all others. Rather, he or she is determined to experience every one. Neither does the sensitive reader direct all of his or her efforts toward substantiating a single response while dismissing all others.

In short, whatever the ethical or logical drawbacks of New Hedonism, it does provide a useful model for reading. The openness to experience that stands as the central tenet of New Hedonism serves as a useful reminder to the reader seeking the fullest possible response to Wilde's narrative. *The Picture of Dorian Gray* offers a wide range of aesthetic pleasure and leaves to the reader the task of remaining open to the aesthetic options it presents. In the concluding chapter of this study, I take up the question of how so many views emerge concurrently in our responses to Wilde's novel.

7

Conclusion

There is only one thing in the world worse than being talked about, and that is not being talked about.

The Picture of Dorian Gray

The commentary on art and interpretation found in Wilde's preface to the novel-length version of *The Picture of Dorian Gray* is an enlightening resource. Because of its unique status as a work inspired by the harsh reactions to the original version of the novel and aimed at illuminating key features of the narrative, the preface is an interpretive guide that enhances understanding without prescribing meaning.

Rather than advocating a single interpretation, it outlines the full imaginative structure of the work, highlighting its diverse elements and suggesting ways to unify them. Thus, by using the preface to set interpretive boundaries, the reader can eschew dependence on a particular point of view and instead embrace the full range of perspectives the narrative puts forward.

Wilde composed the preface in February 1891, and he first published it in March of that year as an independent essay, printed in the

Fortnightly Review under the title "A Preface to *Dorian Gray*." One month later it reappeared under the title "The Preface" as part of the novel-length version of *The Picture of Dorian Gray*.[1] Wilde wrote the preface after the controversy over *Lippincott's* novella version of the work in the summer of 1890; he was clearly trying to mediate the conflict that had arisen when some reviewers found various elements in the story an affront to conventional Victorian sensibilities.

The preface replies directly to many of the specific criticisms of the moral atmosphere of the earlier work. In his attempt to facilitate full understanding, Wilde draws sharp attention to a number of the controlling creative assumptions that emerge only implicitly over the course of the narrative. The preface not only presents Wilde's reflections on the structure of the work that had already appeared but attempts to prepare readers for the expanded version he had recently completed.

Because it was published twice, the preface is that much more authoritative in the interpretations of *The Picture of Dorian Gray* it promotes. In its first appearance in the *Fortnightly Review*, the preface enjoyed an independent position that allowed Wilde to elaborate on views already introduced in the novella-length version of *The Picture of Dorian Gray*. This independence also helped it avoid the appearance of prescriptiveness: The "A" in the title, for example, implies that other, equally valid prefaces might be brought forward. When this preface surfaced again in the expanded version of *The Picture of Dorian Gray*, its position and functions shifted from that of an after-the-fact commentary situated outside the work to that of a compositional element linked, however tenuously, to the narrative. In both aspects, it contributes to the reader's imaginative response to the novel.

The preface also offers a gloss on the creative forces, both internal and external, that shaped Wilde's imagination as he composed the work. The broadly structured commentary on the nature of art, on the functions of criticism, on the work of the artist, and on the attitudes of readers introduces a range of important issues to consider as the reader forms a response to the narrative. Additionally, the preface does not give preference to any of the shifting opinions it expresses but rather leaves the reader with ample scope for alternative interpretations.

At its most fundamental level, the preface discusses the effect of the assumptions about the process of understanding most readers bring to a work of literature. Through its playful inversion of conventional assumptions about reading, the preface challenges the validity of the common tendency to take a single approach to reading and understanding a novel. As an alternative, it outlines a series of interpretive positions that lead to equally plausible but also mutually contradictory views of *The Picture of Dorian Gray*.

The format of the preface presents readers with a fundamental choice: its critical framework simultaneously sustains a number of different interpretive positions and suggests that such an accommodation gives the reader the fullest possible sense of the work. The reader can either adopt a set of unconventional imaginative assumptions or resist the preface's overt invitation and read it in a highly selective fashion—that is, with a single response in mind and suppressing any elements of the work that do not contribute to that response.

The options offered by this structure reflect an artistic condition already familiar in Wilde's canon. Nonetheless, their presentation in the preface subtly alters our expectations about *The Picture of Dorian Gray*. Unlike much of Wilde's previous writing, the preface imaginatively engages the reader not by using paradox (the rhetorical device commonly assumed to inform his writing) but by presenting a series of ambiguities, a succession of very specific and highly provocative statements that involve us in the discourse simply by defining issues rather than by attempting to resolve them.

At the very beginning of the preface, for example, Wilde introduces the question of the status of an artist, and in so doing, he invites the reader to confront the issue of perspective that arises when examining the natures of Dorian, Lord Henry, and Basil Hallward.

> THE artist is the creator of beautiful things.
> To reveal art and conceal the artist is art's aim. (xxxiii)

While these comments seem to be a straightforward definition of the artist and his role, for anyone familiar with the events of *The Picture of*

Dorian Gray they beg several questions. At the most general level, Wilde is raising fundamental issues about the nature and status of beauty, leading us to consider questions that inform the action of *The Picture of Dorian Gray*: whether beauty exists as an independent phenomenon, and whether the elements constituting beauty are stable or fluctuate.

The next statement further unsettles our assumptions about reading, for it seems to contradict the preface's opening lines and to overturn the conventional relationship between the artwork and the artist. How does the reader come to an understanding of these contrasting statements? For instance, should the term "to reveal" be read as synonymous with the act of creation, and conversely, should "to conceal" be read as synonymous with destruction? What in fact do these remarks say about the relation of an artist to his creation? And with all this talk of revelation and concealment, should we begin to wonder whether the act of creation also functions to some extent as an act of interpretation?

The unsettling nature of the issues raised by Wilde's opening remarks underscores the dramatic impact the preface can have on our sense of the act of reading. If, for instance, one balances the importance of artistic creativity as a theme in *The Picture of Dorian Gray* against the preface's unorthodox description of the relationship between art and the artist, one might legitimately feel hard-pressed to decide which character strikes that balance: Basil Hallward must be given credit for painting the picture, but both Basil and Lord Henry contribute to creating or at least to enlivening Dorian's highly complex and beautiful nature, which comes to dominate the novel. Furthermore, through his shaping influence on the physical condition of the painting, Dorian himself seems to assume the contradictory role of both a creator and a negator of beautiful things. What status does this role confer on him? What status, for that matter, does the same role confer on Basil and Lord Henry, who both see themselves reflected in their creations (or re-creations) of Dorian's nature?

After raising questions about the reader's interpretive assumptions in determining the status of characters in the novel, the preface very quickly shifts the focus of its inquiry to the role of the individual in responding to a piece of art. In a wide-ranging survey of different critical postures, Wilde outlines a striking number of alternative positions that can come out of the act of reading.

> The critic is he who can translate into another manner or a new material his impression of beautiful things.
>
> The highest as the lowest form of criticism is a mode of auto-biography.
>
> Those who find ugly meanings in beautiful things are corrupt without being charming. This is a fault.
>
> Those who find beautiful meanings in beautiful things are the cultivated. For these there is hope.
>
> They are the elect to whom beautiful things mean only Beauty. (xxxiii)

Although these remarks raise important issues about how we generate meaning, their very form begs consideration of far more immediate questions about the roles of different individual readers of *The Picture of Dorian Gray*.

In these lines the preface calls on each of us to decide whether we identify ourselves with "the critic"—whom Wilde at times so harshly censures—and if so, what sort of critic we choose to become. Further, we must ask what difference, if any, exists between the critic and any of the rest of us who assume the role of reader. If we see no difference, then how should we respond to the charges Wilde makes against critics? On the other hand, if we do perceive differences between the critic and the reader and we choose to label ourselves readers, what concern, if any, should we have with the function of critics?

Such issues seem perplexing because they threaten the stability of meaning most of us take for granted. However we resolve them, they mark only the first stage of interpretive inquiry presented by the preface. All these initial statements revolve around the same issue: how an individual (whether designated a critic or a reader) forms a response to a piece of art. By identifying a number of alternative reactions and by questioning several conventional assumptions about how we create interpretations, Wilde's remarks leave us far more conscious of the vagaries and gaps in our aesthetic function and far less certain of the logical integrity of our judgments.

Put simply, Wilde's remarks undercut the presumption that meaning resides within the work, to be dug out like gold from a mine. Instead, they point toward the individual reader as the source of a work's meaning, an artificer creating from the materials presented by the author.

The first portion of the preface touches on topics similar to those broached in chapters 5 and 6 of this book: the expectations we bring to a work, and the impact of cultural forces on the interpretations we generate. Wilde is hardly denigrating our efforts to form meaning, but he does recognize the relativity of every reading.

The next few lines introduce a theme that dominates the rest of the preface: how several different interpretive levels often operate simultaneously in a sophisticated work of fiction:

There is no such thing as a moral or an immoral book.
Books are well written, or badly written. That is all. (xxxiii)

On the face of it, this remark is a response to the issues raised by some of the reviewers of the initial version of *The Picture of Dorian Gray* who claimed that the book promoted immorality. Wilde rebuts such assertions by first challenging the basic premise—that values are an inherently important part of any novel—and then by redefining the parameters of the debate according to a purely aesthetic perspective.

Simply not using terms like "moral" and "immoral" seems at first an obvious solution to the problem of overly restrictive interpretations. However, in dismissing the possibility that a work of art has an inherent ethical character, Wilde makes a broader assertion: if one rejects the belief that values are intrinsic to a work of literature, then one must logically discard the assumption that a preeminent meaning exists as well.

Not surprisingly, Wilde reinforces this view in the next lines of the preface, but in a fashion that lets the reader come to such a conclusion. By introducing the concepts of well-written and badly written literature, Wilde reinstates the fundamental problem of the innate makeup of a piece of fiction. Given what has been said about the subjectiveness of the terms "moral" and "immoral," we can hardly accept the idea that words like "well" or "badly" have objective foundations. If both words, then, reflect purely subjective attitudes, the logical conclusion is that two different readers can have very different yet equally valid opinions on the quality of a piece of writing. This in turn reinforces the conclusion that purely personal standards form the basis for all assessments of artistic significance.

In the next few lines, Wilde seems at first glance intent on ignoring the disturbing issues he has just raised and interested instead only in previewing the prose style of the novel to follow. He toys allusively with Shakespeare. He teeters on the brink of contradiction and screams for elaboration and clarification. Nonetheless, buoyed by a supreme self-confidence, he passes sweeping judgments about the response of the Victorian era to key literary terms.

The nineteenth century dislike of Realism is the rage of Caliban seeing his own face in a glass.

The nineteenth century dislike of Romanticism is the rage of Caliban not seeing his own face in a glass. (xxxiii)

Although written in the deceptively straightforward tone of objective certainty, Wilde's words here subtly continue to examine the issue of how a reader forms meaning. They leave the reader (or perhaps the critic, depending on the identity we have claimed) with a formidable task. Shifting from his early general concern with interpretation, Wilde turns our attention to the implications of the critical labels "romanticism" and "realism," used so freely and diversely in many other contexts. Further, once the reader has come to even provisional meanings, he or she must appraise the importance of the remarks themselves.

Through the playful circularity of these complementary declarations, Wilde suggests that either reaction is incorrect. He thus raises the specter of antagonism toward literary movements without giving the reader a clear sense of what the nineteenth century in fact did or should have liked. His comments, however, are more than a flippant dismissal of middle-class values, for they materially strengthen the generally subjective tone of the preface. By this point, Wilde has begun to direct the thoughtful reader away from seeking the best formula for reading the novel and toward consideration of more fundamental issues related to how a reader makes an imaginative response to *The Picture of Dorian Gray*. The preface invites a measure of self-reflexivity in order to understand why one selects a particular interpretation.

The next few lines of the preface seem to break away from this line of inquiry to return to the question of how the artist responds to the raw material of art. Rather than shift our attention away from a view of interpretation to concentrate on the artifact, Wilde here underscores the interdependence of these two components of the aesthetic experience: "The moral life of man forms part of the subject-matter of the artist, but the morality of art consists in the perfect use of an imperfect medium" (xxxiii).

Wilde is emphasizing both the centrality of the inner life of an individual as raw material for the creative act and the transforming power of art. While foregrounding the artist's ability, Wilde nonetheless points up the fact that our perceptions of a particular work influence how we create meaning—that is, the meaning we derive rests in how we perceive the "perfect use of an imperfect medium." Although at first glance these remarks on the function of art seem to revive the issue of morality introduced earlier in the preface, they in fact place even greater emphasis on the relationships between aesthetics and the broad concept of values. Further, they do so in a fashion that overturns any reductive suppositions about art and morality that the statements earlier in the preface may have seemed to endorse.

Additionally, Wilde's return to the concept of morality has important implications for an overview of the preface: he negates the objections of generalizers who say that because he refuses to label art along inherently value-laden lines, he lacks an ethical foundation. He also makes a subtler point by rebutting those who see his writing as inherently value-free or amoral. In fact, his remarks directly acknowledge the presence of morality as he takes up the vexing question of how one deals with its highly subjective nature.

Further, Wilde's sentiments here enforce an important distinction between the influence morality exerts on creative inspiration and the way artistic ethics are revealed through an aesthetic creation. This distinction in turn raises the question of whether these two forms of morality function independently: on the one hand, a public system of commonly held views that the artist employs dispassionately as the medium of expression, and on the other, a private code of personal values intrinsic to the artist's practice of his or her craft. Almost immediately, however, Wilde questions the accuracy of such sharp differentiations.

> No artist desires to prove anything. Even things that are true can be proved.
>
> No artist has ethical sympathies. An ethical sympathy in an artist is an unpardonable mannerism of style. (xxxiii)

These remarks, especially compared with the lines immediately preceding them, evoke a more complicated image of the artist who has created *The Picture of Dorian Gray* and of the reader. By proclaiming a measure of ethical neutrality in the act of representation, Wilde clearly condemns any inclination in the artist—and by extension, in the critic—to bring value judgments to the work. At the same time, this neutral position does not banish moral concerns. In fact, in refusing to privilege any, it draws attention to all.

Wilde attempts here to represent ethics as a force present in every intellectual activity but never dominant in an aesthetically satisfying artistic expression. This leveling gesture also points to the rejection of positions that limit the comprehension of a piece of art to a single interpretive view, for if in the creation of art the artist finds all avenues of inquiry open, one can hardly expect the resulting artwork to evoke a single response.

The next few lines of the preface underscore this attitude with a decentered, impressionistic expression of artistic power. Though somewhat exaggerated, Wilde's description lays down useful criteria for measuring what the best works—like *The Picture of Dorian Gray*—strive to accomplish.

> No artist is ever morbid. The artist can express everything.
> Thought and language are to the artist instruments of an art.
>
> Vice and virtue are to the artist materials for an art. (xxxiii)

Here Wilde acknowledges the variability of imaginative powers and clearly rejects the view that a narrowly defined creativity informs the work of an artist. Furthermore, by highlighting the creative potential in the artist's consciousness, he implicitly challenges the reader wishing to comprehend the artwork to match its imaginative scope.

In the midst of these observations, Wilde retains a clear idea of how far these images of diversity can be extended, and he emphasizes this awareness in the next few lines. From a celebration of the artist's seemingly limitless abilities, Wilde moves into a narrower classification of the ideal modes of expression.

> From the point of view of form, the type of all the arts is the art
> of the musician. From the point of view of feeling, the actor's
> craft is the type. (xxxiii)

The sudden shift introduces a new breadth to the preface as it turns to these other disciplines as models of form and content. And once again, the preface says much more than it seems to at first glance.

It would be a mistake to hold the reductive opinion that Wilde is claiming here that literature occupies a secondary position in terms of aesthetic gratification, or that one stands paralyzed before art, unable to picture the proper mode of response. Rather, the reader can perceive the great subtlety of these observations by recollecting the key issues Wilde emphasizes throughout the preface. In choosing performers of art, not the art media themselves, to embody the highest examples of theme and structure, Wilde separates these ideals from their specific media and uses the performer figures to embody broader commentary.

The form of a musician's routine becomes an abstract entity—a Platonic ideal—not bound by a particular score but rather reflecting a larger structure fundamental to all art. Likewise, singling out an actor's craft as the model for feeling goes beyond using specific dialogue as the benchmark for content. Instead, it brings together the numerous elements that make up the actor's delivery—gesture, intonation, modulation, pace—to underscore the impact of a combination of a range of different points of view.

In the next four lines, Wilde continues to explore the interpretive implications of different popular images of the aesthetic experience, but in a very different tone. The terms "surface," "symbol," and "mirror" sum up a more general concept of creative structure; while scrutinizing the ability of the critic to respond to art and making engagement both at the surface and through the symbol seem a perilous endeavor, Wilde stamps the function of art with ambiguity.

> All art is at once surface and symbol.
> Those who go beneath the surface do so at their peril.
> Those who read the symbol do so at their peril.
> It is the spectator, and not life, that art really mirrors. (xxxiv)

Seeing how these words work in the context of the preface, we understand that Wilde's comments were not simply a gratuitous attack on reviewers, paying them back for harsh assessments of his work. Rather, he was drawing attention to the profound difficulties facing those who adopt a single, regularized response to understanding—either the dual model of musician and actor or the twin images of surface and symbol.

Both modes rework the commonplace concept of art as a mirror held up to illuminate nature. They inform us that while art may mirror the spectator, that gesture does not necessarily reflect the image of a passive observer. In fact, as the reactions of various readers to that familiar concept accumulate, all prior associations with the practiced observer who follows predictable protocols leading to predictable responses quickly break down.

> Diversity of opinion about a work of art shows that the work is new, complex, and vital.
>
> When critics disagree the artist is in accord with himself. (xxxiv)

While not entirely forgiving critics for their trade, Wilde does seem to go a bit easier on them here than earlier in the preface. He recognizes the need for a work to produce a range of responses and acknowledges that a critic willing to set aside conventional expectations to discern multiple views becomes a very different type of individual.

In the midst of this series of apparently conflicting points of view, Wilde ends the preface (having reached no simple conclusion) by refocusing on the act of creation and the resulting artifact:

> We can forgive a man for making a useful thing as long as he does not admire it. The only excuse for making a useless thing is that one admires it intensely.
>
> All art is quite useless. (xxxiv)

In denying the practical side of art, Wilde does more than evoke the image of a frivolous nonconformist. By rejecting the view that art is confined to a specific function, Wilde resists the impulse toward categorical labeling that would contradict the appeals to hold a range of views that run throughout *The Picture of Dorian Gray*. Instead, Wilde's final remarks affirm an unwillingness to restrict the reader's response to his novel. In fact, the preface clearly indicates that Wilde has numerous aesthetic positions that he will bring to our attention over the course of his novel.

At the heart of his preface remarks is Wilde's unwillingness to give preference to the interpretive function of the author over the reader, or vice versa. He sees in the artist the need to create in a variety of forms and on a variety of themes, for the most effective art of necessity appeals to a wide and varied combination of viewers in an assortment of ways. The artist does not use a single perspective to tell the reader what to think but instead provides the reader with a wide range of images and ideas to which he or she responds.

At the same time, Wilde is outlining an equally complex role for the reader-critic. His attacks on the very practice of criticism—at least in the institutional form of a single voice dictating to masses of people the worth of a piece of art—deftly undermine any claims to certitude one might have been tempted to ascribe to any particular critical response. At the same time, as can be seen in the passages below from his essay "The Critic as Artist," Wilde underscored the importance of informed, imaginative, and diverse interpretive responses.

> An age that has no criticism is either an age in which art is immobile, hieratic, and confined to the reproduction of formal types, or an age that possesses no art at all. There have been critical ages that have not been creative, in the ordinary sense of the word, ages in which the spirit of man has sought to set in order the treasures of his treasure-house, to separate the gold from the silver, and the silver from the lead, to count over the jewels, and to give names to the pearls. But there has never been a creative age that has not been critical also. For it is the critical faculty that invents fresh forms.
>
> Criticism is no more to be judged by any low standard of imitation or resemblance than is the work of a poet or sculptor. The

critic occupies the same relation to the world of art that he criti-
cises as the artist does to the visible world of form and colour, or
the unseen world of passion and of thought.

The best that one can say of most modern creative art is that it is
just a little less vulgar than reality, and so the critic, with his fine
sense of distinction and sure instinct of delicate refinement, will
prefer to look into the silver mirror or through the woven veil,
and will turn his eyes away from the chaos and clamour of actual
existence, though the mirror be tarnished and the veil be torn. His
sole aim is to chronicle his own impressions. It is for him that pictures are painted, books written, and marble hewn into form.[2]

By outlining in broad strokes the various reactions criticism can make,
Wilde resists both the automatic subordination and elevation of that
function. Rather, he shows its creative capacity to make clear the
dynamic potential of both reader and artist.

Perhaps most significantly, Wilde employs the act of reading his
preface to shape our approach to *The Picture of Dorian Gray*. After
experiencing the interpretive freedom offered by this discourse, the
reader might legitimately wonder about the wisdom of returning to a
restricted conventional approach to *The Picture of Dorian Gray*. That
is to say, if we take seriously both the formal and thematic unortho-
doxy of the preface, we become de facto inclined to sustain simultaneous multiple readings even before we begin the narrative. The preface
teaches us how to read like New Hedonists.

The preface accomplishes this by emphasizing several fundamental and complementary points about the act of reading, grounded in
the assumption that its primary function is the pursuit of pleasure. It
follows from that basic view that the most satisfying interpretations of
The Picture of Dorian Gray seek only to increase that pleasure. Thus,
Wilde implies in the preface, the most effective reading of the novel is
characterized by both selfishness and dependence—it is not one seeking some disassociated reward for finding the hidden meaning buried
beneath the verbiage but rather one that always endeavors to enhance
the direct satisfaction produced by our contact with the work.

Seeing reading as an act of self-gratification leads us to reject traditional, single-minded interpretations of *The Picture of Dorian Gray* that consider only those elements of the narrative that support their narrow contentions. Instead, we must embrace a much less disciplined but ultimately much more satisfying approach. That is, we must forsake the certitude offered by exclusionary readings and give up efforts to impose intellectual and imaginative closure on our endeavors.

As I have emphasized throughout this study, such a project, while relatively easy to outline, proves very difficult to put into practice. We do not easily give up the conventional inclinations that have conditioned our thinking for so long, and the mere promise of increased aesthetic pleasure does not always seem to justify the added effort demanded by new approaches. Nonetheless, if we are to appreciate the full imaginative potential of *The Picture of Dorian Gray*, we need to accept the process of multiplicity that Wilde's preface shows we can sustain.

The truly difficult aspect of this approach lies not in apprehending Wilde's diverse and sophisticated modes of discourse. Nor is it setting in motion a new form of reading. Rather, it lies in each reader's ability to overcome habitual forms of interpretation. To implement pluralistic interpretation, we need only remain open to the possibilities of alternative views and they will emerge. What we must strive toward, then, is an imaginative pluralism like the combination outlined by Wilde in a letter of 12 February 1892 to his friend Ralph Payne:

> I am so glad you like that strange coloured book of mine: it contains much of me in it. Basil Hallward is what I think I am: Lord Henry what the world thinks me: Dorian what I would like to be—in other ages, perhaps. (*LOW*, 352)

Notes and References

Chapter 1

1. The intellectual legacy of Lytton Strachey's *Eminent Victorians* has proven difficult to overcome. As recently as the 1950s, critics approaching the period, while acknowledging its range of features, still treated it as a more or less monolithic entity. See W. E. Houghton, *The Victorian Frame of Mind, 1830–1870* (New Haven, Conn.: Yale University Press, 1957) and Jerome Buckley, *The Victorian Temper: A Study in Literary Culture* (Cambridge, Mass.: Harvard University Press, 1969). The monolithic perspective was radically reassessed in Steven Marcus's pioneering study *The Other Victorians: A Study of Sexuality and Pornography in Mid-Nineteenth-Century England* (New York: Basic Books, 1966). It survives, however, most recently in studies reflecting both the breadth and diversity of Victorian society, such as Richard D. Altick, *The Presence of the Present: Topics of the Day in the Victorian Novel* (Columbus: Ohio State University Press, 1991). The highly idiosyncratic nature of nineteenth-century England is revealed in Regenia Gagnier, *Subjectivities: A History of Self-Representation in Britain, 1832–1920* (New York: Oxford University Press, 1991).

2. The nation of Ireland, while putatively on an equal footing with Britain since the 1801 Act of Union, in fact stood as little more than another colonial outpost of the empire. For a clear delineation of this paradox and its impact on Irish writers, see Marguerite Harkness, *A Portrait of the Artist as a Young Man: Voices of the Text* (Boston: Twayne Publishers, 1990), 1–6.

3. See Richard Ellmann's biography (*Oscar Wilde* [New York: Knopf, 1988], hereafter cited in the text) on Wilde's temperament.

4. Quoted in Ellmann, *Oscar Wilde* (45), from a satirical piece on Wilde in the *Oxford and Cambridge Undergraduates' Journal*, 27 February 1876.

5. Oscar Wilde, *The Letters of Oscar Wilde*, ed. Rupert Hart-Davis (New York: Harcourt, Brace & World, 1962), 53, hereafter cited in the text as *LOW*.

6. See, for example, Ellmann, *Oscar Wilde*, 37–100; and Richard Pine, *Oscar Wilde* (New York: Gill and Macmillan, 1983), 17ff.

7. Quoted in *The Oxford Illustrated History of English Literature*, ed. Pat Rogers (Oxford: Oxford University Press, 1990), 379.

8. André Gide, *Oscar Wilde: In Memoriam (Reminiscences) de Profundis*, trans. Bernard Frechtman (New York: Philological Library, 1949), 16.

9. Quoted from a letter published in *The World* (17 November 1886), reprinted in Ellmann, *Oscar Wilde*, 273–74.

10. Several critics have devoted a good deal of energy to the question of which man exerted the more lasting influence. Richard Ellmann argued most forcefully for the presence in Wilde's consciousness of an ongoing struggle between the ideas of Ruskin and Pater. See his "Overtures to *Salomé*," in *Oscar Wilde: A Collection of Critical Essays*, ed. Richard Ellmann (Englewood Cliffs, N.J.: Prentice-Hall, 1969), 73–91. Philip E. Smith II and Michael S. Helfand continue this argument in *Oscar Wilde's Oxford Notebooks: A Portrait of Mind in the Making* (New York: Oxford University Press, 1989), 10–17.

Chapter 2

1. These writings are often grouped together under the terms modernism and postmodernism. Though variously defined, certain key features obtain in any of the definitions of these terms. Literary modernism refers to writing that foregrounds stylistic experimentation, denies the importance of closure, openly questions the efficacy of social institutions—like the family, religion, and nationalism—and makes the individual (especially when that individual is an artist) rather than societal norms the source of ethical judgments. These features hold for literary postmodernism with the exception of the last: in the decentered postmodern world, no person or institution can pass valid ethical judgments. For detailed explanations of modernism and postmodernism, see Terry Eagleton, *Critical Theory: An Introduction* (Minneapolis: University of Minnesota Press, 1984), and Linda Hutcheon, *A Poetics of Postmodernism: History, Theory, Fiction* (New York: Routledge, 1988).

2. Wilde first published the preface separately. It appeared in the March 1891 issue of the *Fortnightly Review* under the title "A Preface to Dorian Gray," and it was intended as a rebuttal of the harsh criticisms of the *Lippincott's Monthly Magazine* version of the novel published the previous year. (Those attacks are discussed in chapter 3 of this study.)

3. Richard Ellmann, ed., *Letters of James Joyce*, vol. 2 (New York: Viking Press, 1966), 150.

4. Quoted in *The Picture of Dorian Gray*, ed. Isobel Murray (Oxford: Oxford University Press, 1974), 227. For a full sense of Pater's aesthetics, see his work *The Renaissance: Studies in Art and Poetry*, especially the 1888

revised edition's conclusion, which is reprinted in Murray's edition of *The Picture of Dorian Gray*.

Chapter 3

1. Quoted in Oscar Wilde, *Oscar Wilde, Art and Morality: A Defence of* The Picture of Dorian Gray, ed. Stuart Mason (London: J. Jacobs, 1908), 17; reprinted in *Oscar Wilde: The Critical Heritage*, ed. Karl Beckson (London: Routledge & Kegan Paul, 1970), 68–69, hereafter cited in the text as *Critical Heritage*.

2. See especially Wilde's letters to the editors of the journals in which these reviews appeared, reprinted in *LOW* (259, 260, 263, 264, 266, 268).

3. For complete reprints of these reviews, see Mason, *Art and Morality*, 101–24. A portion of Hawthorne's piece and Pater's complete review appear in *Critical Heritage*, 74–80 and 83–86.

4. For detailed assessments of these changes, see Isobel Murray, "Some Elements in the Composition of *The Picture of Dorian Gray*," *Durham University Journal* 64 (January 1972): 220–31. See also Murray's introduction to the Oxford edition of *The Picture of Dorian Gray* and the series of letters that appeared in the *(London) Times Literary Supplement*, 26 June–13 September 1974. The most detailed work in this area is found in Donald L. Lawler, *An Inquiry into Oscar Wilde's Revisions of* The Picture of Dorian Gray (New York: Garland, 1988). See also Donald L. Lawler, "Oscar Wilde's First Manuscript of *The Picture of Dorian Gray*," *Studies in Bibliography* 25 (1972): 125–35, and "The Revisions of *Dorian Gray*," *Victorians Institute Journal* 3 (1974): 21–36.

5. Wilde not only attracted the attention of critics in America and England but also held the interest of a succession of German scholars. Although their work falls outside the purview of this study, those interested in additional information on German interpretations of *The Picture of Dorian Gray* should consult Ian Fletcher and John Stokes, "Oscar Wilde," in *Anglo-Irish Literature: A Review of Research*, ed. Richard J. Finneran (New York: Modern Language Association of America, 1976), 48–137. See also their supplement to this entry, "Oscar Wilde," in *Recent Research on Anglo-Irish Writers*, ed. Richard J. Finneran (New York: Modern Language Association of America, 1983), 21–47.

6. A number of fine bibliographers—Ian Fletcher and John Stokes, Karl Beckson, E. H. Mikhail, Norbert Kohl, and Ian Small—have meticulously charted the evolution of Wilde criticism, and their complementary studies provide ample evidence of such a trend: Karl Beckson, ed., *Oscar Wilde: The Critical Heritage* (London: Routledge & Kegan Paul, 1970); E. H. Mikhail, *Oscar Wilde: An Annotated Bibliography of Criticism* (London: Macmillan, 1978); Norbert Kohl, *Oscar Wilde: The Works of a Conformist Rebel*, trans.

David Henry Wilson (Cambridge: Cambridge University Press, 1989); Ian Small, *Oscar Wilde Revalued: An Essay on New Materials and Methods of Research* (Greensboro, NC: ELT Press, 1993).

7. Arthur Ransome, *Oscar Wilde: A Critical Study* (London: Martin Secker, 1912). Lord Alfred Bruce Douglas wrote a number of memoirs, more or less changing his account with each one. See *Oscar Wilde and Myself* (London: John Long, 1914); *A Letter from Lord Alfred Douglas on André Gide's Lies about Himself and Oscar Wilde. Set Forth with Comments by Robert Harborough Sherard* (Calvi, Corsica: Vindex Publishing Co., 1933); *Without Apology* (London: Martin Secker, 1938); and *Oscar Wilde: A Summing-Up* (London: Duckworth, 1940). Harris referred to Wilde in various autobiographical works. The most extended study appears in Frank Harris, *Oscar Wilde: His Life and Confessions* (Garden City, N.Y.: Garden City Publishing Co., 1930).

8. See Robert Sherard, *Oscar Wilde: The Story of an Unhappy Friendship* (London: privately printed, 1902; London: Greening, 1905); *The Life of Oscar Wilde* (London: T. Werner Laurie, 1906); *André Gide's Wicked Lies about the Late Mr. Oscar Wilde in Algiers in January, 1895* (Calvi, Corsica: Vindex Publishing Co., 1933); *Oscar Wilde, "Drunkard and Swindler": A Reply to George Bernard Shaw, Dr. G. J. Renier, Frank Harris, etc.* (Calvi, Corsica: Vindex Publishing Co., 1933); and *Oscar Wilde Twice Defended from André Gide's Wicked Lies and Frank Harris's Cruel Libels* (Chicago: Argus, 1934).

9. Ian Fletcher and John Stokes, "Oscar Wilde," in *Anglo-Irish Literature: A Review of Research,* ed. Richard J. Finneran (New York: Modern Language Association of America, 1976), 48–135.

10. Ellmann, *Oscar Wilde.* Nonetheless, even Ellmann at times succumbs to forming analogies between the life Wilde lived and the art he created that oversimplify the aesthetic features of Wilde's writings and truncate the process of interpretive understanding. David Norris, for example, while praising Ellmann's general treatment of Wilde, has expressed the view that a limited comprehension of Wilde's homosexuality circumscribed Ellmann's sense of Wilde's writings (remarks at 13th International James Joyce Symposium, 1993). In a succinct critique of Ellmann's approach, but in an even harsher vein, Peter Costello derides what he calls "Ellmann's venereal enthusiasms" and sharply critiques "the syphilitic theme of [Ellmann's] book," which ignores basic medical evidence in favor of a sensationalized story (review of *"What Did I Die Of?"* by J. B. Lyons, *Irish Literary Supplement* 12, no. 1 [Spring 1993]: 18). For both Norris and Costello, reductive either-or approaches insinuate simplistic polarities into the discourse that threaten to oversimplify a reader's responses to Wilde and his canon. See also Small, *Oscar Wilde Revalued,* 17–18.

11. Robert Boyle, S. J., "Oscar Wilde," *Dictionary of Literary Biography—British Novelists, 1890–1929: Traditionalists,* vol. 34 (Detroit: Gale Research, 1985), 317–18.

12. Frances Winwar, *Oscar Wilde and the Yellow Nineties* (New York: Harper and Bros., 1940).

13. See, for example, Vyvyan Holland, *Oscar Wilde: A Pictorial Biography* (London: Thames & Hudson, 1966); and Martin Fido, *Oscar Wilde* (New York: Viking Press, 1973).

14. J. E. Chamberlin, *Ripe Was the Drowsy Hour: The Age of Oscar Wilde* (New York: Seabury Press, 1977); Regenia Gagnier, *Idylls of the Marketplace: Oscar Wilde and the Victorian Public* (Stanford, Calif.: Stanford University Press, 1986).

15. Christopher Nassaar, *Into the Demon Universe* (New Haven, Conn.: Yale University Press, 1974); Philip K. Cohen, *The Moral Vision of Oscar Wilde* (Rutherford, N.J.: Fairleigh Dickinson University Press, 1978.) Other examples of this approach to *The Picture of Dorian Gray* are Ted R. Spivey, "Damnation and Salvation in *The Picture of Dorian Gray*," *Boston University Studies in English* 4 (1960): 162–70; and Dominic Manganiello, "Ethics and Aesthetics in *The Picture of Dorian Gray*," *Canadian Journal of Irish Studies* 9 (December 1983): 25–33.

16. Epifanio San Juan, Jr., *The Art of Oscar Wilde* (Princeton, N.J.: Princeton University Press, 1967). Of the subsequent studies along the same lines, two of the best are Robert Keefe, "Artist and Model in *The Picture of Dorian Gray*," *Studies in the Novel* 5 (1973): 63–70; and Donald B. Dickson, "'In a Mirror That Mirrors the Soul': Masks and Mirrors in *Dorian Gray*," *English Literature in Transition* 26 (1983): 5–15.

17. See, for example, Houston Baker, "A Tragedy of the Artist: *The Picture of Dorian Gray*," *Nineteenth-Century Fiction* 24 (1969): 349–55; Dominick Rossi, "Parallels in Wilde's *The Picture of Dorian Gray* and Goethe's *Faust*," *College Language Association Journal* 13 (1969): 188–91; and Spivey, "Damnation and Salvation in *Dorian Gray*."

18. Eve Kosofsky Sedgwick, *Between Men: English Literature and Male Homosocial Desire* (New York: Columbia University Press, 1986); Richard Dellamora, "Representation and Homophobia in *The Picture of Dorian Gray*," *Victorian Newsletter* 73 (1988): 28–31; Ed Cohen, "Writing Gone Wilde: Homoerotic Desire in the Closet of Repression," *PMLA* 102 (October 1987): 801–13.

19. Camille A. Paglia, "Oscar Wilde and the English Epicene," *Raritan* 4, no. 3 (1985): 85–109; Gagnier, *Idylls of the Marketplace*.

20. Small, *Oscar Wilde Revalued*, 168–70; Kerry Powell, "Tom, Dick, and Dorian Gray: Magic-Picture Mania in Late Victorian Fiction," *Philological Quarterly* 62 (Spring 1983): 147–70.

21. Oscar Wilde, *The Importance of Being Earnest: A Trivial Comedy for Serious People, in Four Acts as Originally Written by Oscar Wilde*, 2 vols. (New York: New York Public Library, 1956).

22. John Espy, "Resources for Wilde Studies at the Clark Library," in *Oscar Wilde: Two Approaches* (Los Angeles: William Andrews Clark Memorial Library, University of California at Los Angeles, 1977), 25–48.

Chapter 4

1. Wilde's fellow Irishman, James Joyce, was also aware of the distinctions created by articles and by the various terms designating a painting when he chose to entitle his novel *A Portrait of the Artist as a Young Man*.

2. Most critical responses to Wilde's novel, while covering a wide range of approaches, maintain the primacy of a single dominant point of view. The following book-length studies are fairly representative of different modes of interpretations, and their titles underscore a range of possible perspectives: Kohl, *Oscar Wilde: The Works of a Conformist Rebel*; Gagnier, *Idylls of the Marketplace: Oscar Wilde and the Victorian Audience*; Cohen, *The Moral Vision of Oscar Wilde*; Chamberlin, *Ripe Was the Drowsy Hour: The Age of Oscar Wilde*; Donald H. Ericksen, *Oscar Wilde* (New York: Twayne, 1977); Nassaar, *Into the Demon Universe: A Literary Exploration of Oscar Wilde*.

3. Not every critic would agree with this approach. Good examples of interpretations that emphasize the homosexual aspects of *Dorian Gray* are: Cohen, "Writing Gone Wilde: Homoerotic Desire in the Closet of Representation"; and Jonathan Dollimore, "Different Desires: Subjectivity and Transgression in Wilde and Gide," *Genders* 2 (Summer 1988): 24–41. This view, however, illustrates my point that any determinedly linear approach inevitably loses touch with elements in the novel that do not sustain its argument.

4. Some critics, of course, have argued that Dorian changes for the worse because of the force of art. See, for example, Dickson, "'In a Mirror That Mirrors the Soul': Masks and Mirrors in *Dorian Gray*." That sort of linear interpretation, however, narrowly casts Dorian in the role of Narcissus and is diametrically opposed to the multiple forms of reading I am suggesting.

Chapter 5

1. For some, the role of ethics in literary criticism remains a problematic issue, and its relation to aesthetic response is still open to debate. See, for example, Edward A. Watson, "Wilde's Iconoclastic Classicism: 'The Critic as Artist'," *English Literature in Transition* 27 (1984): 225–35; and William E. Buckler, "Antinomianism or Anarchy? A Note on Oscar Wilde's 'Pen, Pencil and Poison,'" *Victorian Newsletter* 78 (1990): 1–3. J. Hillis Miller has sought to clarify the issues in *The Ethics of Reading* (New York: Columbia University Press, 1987); see also his *Versions of Pygmalion* (Cambridge, Mass.: Harvard University Press, 1990). Miller's assessment of how ethics shapes aesthetic

views is far more prescriptive than my own, but I still see value in his articulation of the issue.

2. Not every critic would support the view that ethics and aesthetics function intradependently in *The Picture of Dorian Gray*. For an elaboration of the view that the novel "examines frankly the consequences of substituting an aesthetic for an ethical conscience," see Dominic Manganiello, "Ethics and Aesthetics in *The Picture of Dorian Gray*," *Canadian Journal of Irish Studies* 9 (December 1983): 25–33.

3. For a more detailed look at the relationship between ethical views and literary interpretation, see Robert Hoopes, *Right Reason in the English Renaissance* (Cambridge, Mass.: Harvard University Press, 1962). Although Hoopes wrote this study over 30 years ago, it remains a useful scholarly survey of the topic.

4. Wilde's specific views about philosophy and philosophers were diverse and discursive. Nonetheless, an interesting range of observations, all the more tantalizing for their brevity, are collected in his university notes. For details, see Smith and Helfand, *Oscar Wilde's Oxford Notebooks*.

5. Sporadic articulations of such a view have occurred, of course, throughout history. It was not, however, until the rise of existentialism in the middle of the twentieth century that this perspective gained legitimacy as an alternative school of thought.

6. Richard Ellmann points out this connection between Wilde and Pater, as well as noting the influence of Ruskin, in his essay "Overtures to Salomé," in *Oscar Wilde: A Collection of Critical Essays*, ed. Richard Ellmann (Englewood Cliffs, N.J.: Prentice-Hall, 1969). In my opinion, Ellmann's view that "in *Dorian Gray* the Pater side of Wilde's thought is routed, though not deprived of fascination" (90) is reductive. Nonetheless, he rightly draws attention to the impact of both men on Wilde's aesthetics.

7. Murray, *The Picture of Dorian Gray*, 227–28.

8. Such views are reflected in the contemporary newspaper reviews of the novel already mentioned. Several recent critical works provide traditional moral readings of *The Picture of Dorian Gray*, among them, Nassaar's *Into the Demon Universe*. Philip Cohen takes a similar approach in *The Moral Vision of Oscar Wilde*. The same sort of ethical reading, but from a very different perspective, the social hermeneutics of gay criticism, appears in Ed Cohen's "Writing Gone Wilde," and Dollimore's "Different Desires." In chapter 6, I discuss the interpretive challenges presented by this range of readings.

9. This process calls to mind Roland Barthes's "writerly text," which demands the active engagement of the reader to complete its meaning. For a full discussion of this concept, see Roland Barthes, *S/Z*, trans. Richard Miller (New York: Hill and Wang, 1974).

Chapter 6

1. There are, of course, a number of useful interpretive models offered by critics whom Chandra Mukerji and Michael Schudson (in *Rethinking Popular Culture: Contemporary Perspectives in Cultural Studies,* ed. Chandra Mukerji and Michael Schudson [Berkeley: University of California Press, 1991], 432–64) characterize as attentive "to the sensual nature of the reading process" (48). See, for example, Roland Barthes's "Written Clothing" and Michel Foucault's "What Is an Author," both of which appear in the cited volume. The potential of their methodologies, however, remains to be developed.

2. Perhaps the clearest delineation of the complex sexual mores of the Victorian era appears in the watershed study by Steven Marcus, *The Other Victorians: A Study of Sexuality and Pornography in Mid-Nineteenth-Century England* (New York: Basic Books, 1966).

3. See chapter 3, notes 1–3.

4. Nassaar, *Into the Demon Universe,* 37–72.

5. Ibid., 72.

6. Cohen, *The Moral Vision of Oscar Wilde,* 105–55.

7. Ibid., 116, 118.

8. Rupert Croft-Cooke, *The Unrecorded Life of Oscar Wilde* (New York: David McKay Co., 1972), 112.

9. See, for example, Rodney Shewan, *Oscar Wilde: Art and Egoism* (New York: Barnes and Noble Books, 1977), 112–13.

10. Most adherents of this view do not limit themselves to *The Picture of Dorian Gray* but see throughout Wilde's canon evidence of didactic defense of homosexuality. See, for example, Camille A. Paglia, "Oscar Wilde and the English Epicene," *Raritan* 4, no. 3 (Winter 1985): 85–109; Dollimore, "Different Desires"; Cohen, "Writing Gone Wilde."

11. An excellent analysis of this shift in critical perspectives appears in Small, *Oscar Wilde Revalued,* esp. 155–79.

12. Gagnier, *Idylls of the Marketplace,* 62.

13. For example, Winwar, *Oscar Wilde and the Yellow Nineties*; Chamberlin, *Ripe Was the Drowsy Hour*; Ellmann, *Oscar Wilde.*

14. For a complete discussion, see my essay "Picturing Dorian Gray: Resistant Readings in Wilde's Novel," *English Literature in Transition* 35, no. 1 (1992): 7–25.

15. For what is still the most detailed review of nineteenth-century representations of the dandy, see Ellen Moers, *The Dandy: Brummell to Beerbohm* (Lincoln: University of Nebraska Press, 1960).

16. Gagnier also sees elements of the dandy in her readings of *The Picture of Dorian Gray,* and both she and I have used Moers's study as a starting point for our interpretations. We differ, however, very markedly in where

we situate the dandy in relation to society and in consequence come to very different conclusions. For a more detailed view of my approach, see "From Beau Brummell to Lady Bracknell: Re-viewing the Dandy in *The Importance of Being Earnest*," *Victorians Institute Journal* 21 (1993): 119–42.

Chapter 7

1. Ellmann, *Oscar Wilde*, 335.

2. Oscar Wilde, *Intentions* (London: James P. Osgood McIlvane & Co., 1891), 123, 136, 138–39.

Bibliography

Primary Sources

The Ballad of Reading Gaol. London: Smithers, 1898.

The Complete Works of Oscar Wilde. Edited by Vyvyan Holland. London: Collins, 1948.

De Profundis. London: Methuen, 1905; New York and London: Putnam, 1905. The complete, authoritative version appears in *LOW*.

The Duchess of Padua: A Tragedy of the XVI Century, Written in Paris in the XIX Century. New York: privately printed, 1883.

Essays of Oscar Wilde. Edited by Hesketh Pearson. London: Methuen, 1950.

First Collected Edition of the Works of Oscar Wilde. Edited by Robert Ross. Vols. 1–11, 13–14. London: Methuen, 1908; Boston: Luce, 1910. Vol. 10. Paris: Carrington, 1908. The *Second Collected Edition*, also edited by Ross, was published in 1909 (vols. 1–12), 1910 (vol. 13), and 1912 (vol. 14).

The Happy Prince and Other Tales. London: Nutt, 1888; Boston: Roberts, 1888.

A House of Pomegranates. London: Osgood, McIlvaine, 1891; New York: Dodd, Mead, 1892.

The Ideal Husband. London: Smithers, 1899.

The Importance of Being Earnest: A Trivial Comedy for Serious People. London: Smithers, 1899.

Intentions. London: Osgood, McIlvane & Co., 1891; New York: Dodd, Mead, 1891.

Lady Windermere's Fan: A Play about a Good Woman. London: Mathews & Lane, Bodley Head, 1893.

116

Bibliography

The Letters of Oscar Wilde. Edited by Rupert Hart-Davis. New York: Harcourt, Brace & World, 1962.

Literary Criticism of Oscar Wilde. Edited by Stanley Weintraub. Lincoln: University of Nebraska Press, 1968.

Lord Arthur Savile's Crime and Other Stories. London: Osgood, McIlvaine, 1891; New York: Dodd, Mead, 1891.

More Letters of Oscar Wilde. Edited by Rupert Hart-Davis. New York: Vanguard, 1985.

Oscar Wilde, Art and Morality: A Defence of The Picture of Dorian Gray. Edited by Stuart Mason. London: J. Jacobs, 1908.

Oscar Wilde: Complete Shorter Fiction. Oxford: Oxford University Press, 1979.

Oscar Wilde: De Profundis and the Ballad of Reading Gaol. New York: Avon Books, 1964.

The Picture of Dorian Gray. London, New York, Melbourne: Ward, Lock, 1891.

The Picture of Dorian Gray. Edited by Isobel Murray. Oxford: Oxford University Press, 1974.

Poems. London: Bogue, 1881; Boston: Roberts, 1881.

The Portrait of Mr. W.H. Portland, Maine: Mosher, 1901.

Salomé: Drame en un acte. Paris: Libraire de l'Art Indépendent, 1893; London: Mathews & Lane, Bodley Head, 1893. Published in English as *Salomé: A Tragedy in One Act*. Translated by Alfred Douglas. London: Elkin Mathews & John Lane, 1894; Boston: Copeland & Day, 1894.

The Soul of Man [under Socialism]. London: privately printed, 1895.

The Sphinx. London: Mathews & Lane, Bodley Head, 1894; Boston: Copeland & Day, 1894.

Vera; or, The Nihilists: A Drama. London: privately printed, 1880.

A Woman of No Importance. London: Lane, Bodley Head, 1894.

The Writings of Oscar Wilde. Edited by Isobel Murray. Oxford University Press, 1989.

Secondary Sources

Albert, John. "The Christ of Oscar Wilde." *American Benedictine Review* 39 (December 1988): 372–403. A highly sympathetic examination of Wilde's life and writings. Pays particular attention to the manifestations throughout his canon of Wilde's view of Christ.

Auden, W. H. "An Improbable Life." In *Oscar Wilde: De Profundis and The Ballad of Reading Gaol*, 3–30. New York: Avon Books, 1962. An examination of Wilde's life as illuminated by his correspondence, especially his long prison letter, *De Profundis*.

Baker, Houston. "A Tragedy of the Artist: *The Picture of Dorian Gray*." *Nineteenth Century Fiction* 24 (1969): 349–55. A thoughtful archetypal approach to Wilde's novel that evokes inevitable analogues to the Faust story.

Bashford, Bruce. "Oscar Wilde and Subjective Criticism." *English Literature in Transition* 21 (1978): 218–34. A provocative essay that focuses on the "subjectivist theory of criticism" that pervades Wilde's art. Bashford explores the difficulties many critics have in comprehending the implications of such subjectivity.

Beckson, Karl, ed. *Oscar Wilde: The Critical Heritage*. London: Routledge & Kegan Paul, 1970. A useful survey of a range of critical responses to Wilde's work; especially valuable for its collection of early interpretations of Wilde's writings.

Boyle, S. J., Robert. "Oscar Wilde." *Dictionary of Literary Biography—British Novelists, 1890–1929: Traditionalists*. Vol. 34, 317–18. Detroit: Gale Research, 1985. A scholarly and critical overview of Wilde's life and work. Boyle's succinct prose and insightful critical abilities make this essay one of the best available introductions to Wilde and his canon.

Chamberlin, J. E. *Ripe Was the Drowsy Hour: The Age of Oscar Wilde*. New York: Seabury Press, 1977. A pioneering effort to explore the cultural context of Wilde's work. An idiosyncratic tone occasionally disrupts Chamberlin's social criticism of the period, but overall the study offers a useful commentary on Wilde's writing.

Cohen, Ed. "Writing Gone Wilde: Homoerotic Desire in the Closet of Repression." *PMLA* 102 (October 1987): 801–13. A polemical view of the influence of homosexuality on Wilde's writing. This essay is an important reassessment of Wilde's work, but it also suffers from a didactic narrowness that leads Cohen to overlook obvious interpretive alternatives.

Cohen, Philip K. *The Moral Vision of Oscar Wilde*. Rutherford, N.J.: Fairleigh Dickinson University Press; London: Associated University Presses, 1978. An interpretive survey of Wilde's canon that offers good breadth but is limited by a prescriptive moral view.

Dellamora, Richard. "Representation and Homophobia in *The Picture of Dorian Gray*." *Victorian Newsletter* 73 (1988): 28–31. A pioneering work that draws on an emerging body of gender criticism to articulate aspects of gay aesthetics relevant to readings of Wilde's novel.

Dickson, Donald B. "'In a Mirror That Mirrors the Soul': Masks and Mirrors in *Dorian Gray*." *English Literature in Transition* 26 (1983): 5–15. An examination of Wilde's novel that focuses on analogues with the story of Narcissus.

Dollimore, Jonathan. "Different Desires: Subjectivity and Transgression in Wilde and Gide." *Genders* 2 (Summer 1988): 24–41. Although this work does not directly treat *The Picture of Dorian Gray*, it is a good example of the gender criticism of Wilde's work that first came to prominence in the 1980s.

Douglas, Lord Alfred Bruce. *Oscar Wilde and Myself*. London: John Long, 1914; New York: Duffield, 1914. The first of a series of memoirs of Wilde that Douglas published. As with the other works by Douglas listed below, the accuracy of his memoirs is dubious. Because of Douglas's close association with Wilde, they remain important to any effort to understand Wilde's creative life.

———. *The Autobiography of Lord Alfred Douglas*. London: Secker, 1929. Published as *My Friendship with Oscar Wilde*. New York: Coventry, 1932.

———. *Without Apology*. London: Martin Secker, 1938; Toronto: Ryerson, 1938.

———. *Oscar Wilde: A Summing-Up*. London: Duckworth, 1940.

Ellmann, Richard. *Oscar Wilde*. New York: Knopf, 1988. A good synthesis of what is known of Wilde's life and times. Some readers may find that this biography offers far more detail than they wish to have, but Ellmann's felicitous prose style makes accounts of even the most banal events a pleasure to read.

Ericksen, Donald H. *Oscar Wilde*. Boston: G. K. Hall, 1977. A critical survey of Wilde's writings that offers a very good and refreshingly straightforward summary of conventional interpretations of the canon.

Espy, John. "Resources for Wilde Studies at the Clark Library." In *Oscar Wilde: Two Approaches*, 25–48. Los Angeles: William Andrews Clark Memorial Library, 1977. A detailed examination of the Wilde manuscript material available at the William Andrews Clark Library. Espy offers an especially useful analysis of *The Picture of Dorian Gray* manuscripts and typescripts.

Fletcher, Ian, and John Stokes. "Oscar Wilde." In *Anglo-Irish Literature: A Review of Research*, edited by Richard J. Finneran, 48–135. New York: Modern Language Association of America, 1976. A bibliography of primary and secondary sources and manuscript locations that serves as a useful supplement to E. H. Mikhail's work.

Gagnier, Regenia. *Idylls of the Marketplace: Oscar Wilde and the Victorian Public*. Stanford, Calif.: Stanford University Press, 1986. A thoughtful analysis of Wilde's writings, considered within their cultural context. A didactic undercurrent punctuates Gagnier's criticism, but the sharpness of her interpretive insight offsets any narrowness of scope produced by her polemicism.

————, ed. *Critical Essays on Oscar Wilde*. New York: G. K. Hall, 1991. A good collection of a range of approaches to Wilde's writings, including a number of interesting approaches to *The Picture of Dorian Gray*. Also offers several fine examples of interpretations derived from cultural criticism.

Gide, André. *Oscar Wilde: In Memoriam (Reminiscences) de Profundis*. Translated by Bernard Frechtman. New York: Philological Library, 1949. Gide's anecdotal recollection of his friendship with Wilde.

Harley, Bruce. "Wilde's 'Decadence' and the Positivist Tradition." *Victorian Studies* 28 (1985): 215–29. A scholarly effort to situate Wilde's aesthetics within nineteenth-century philosophic thought.

Harris, Frank. *Oscar Wilde: His Life and Confessions*. Garden City, N.Y.: Garden City Publishing, 1930. An engrossing but totally unreliable account of Wilde's life. Its appendices include "The Full and Final Confession by Lord Alfred Douglas" and George Bernard Shaw's "My Memories of Oscar Wilde."

Holland, Vyvyan. *Oscar Wilde: A Pictoral Biography*. London: Thames & Hudson, 1966. A good introduction to Wilde's life and times by his younger son.

Hyde, H. Montgomery. *The Trials of Oscar Wilde*. London: William Hodge, 1948. Published as *The Tree Trials of Oscar Wilde*. New York: University Books, 1956. Provides a good account of Wilde's legal problems.

————. *Oscar Wilde: The Aftermath*. London: Methuen, 1963; New York: Farrar, Straus, 1963. An account of the circumstances surrounding Wilde's arrest, his time in jail, and his final years.

————. *Oscar Wilde: A Biography*. New York: Farrar, Straus, and Giroux, 1975. A good synthesis of Hyde's previous work on Wilde.

Jullian, Philippe. *Oscar Wilde*. Translated by Violet Wyndham. New York: Viking Press, 1969. A highly idiosyncratic approach to Wilde's life.

Keefe, Robert. "Artist and Model in *The Picture of Dorian Gray*." *Studies in the Novel* 5 (1973): 63–70. A detailed examination of the relationship between Basil Hallward and Dorian Gray.

Kohl, Norbert. *Oscar Wilde: The Works of a Conformist Rebel*. Translated by David Henry Wilson. Cambridge: Cambridge University Press, 1989. Originally published in German in 1980 as *Oscar Wilde: Das literarische Werk zwischen Provokation und Anpassung*. The most detailed study of Wilde's work and of Wilde criticism to date. At times Kohl's thoroughness clots his prose, but his scholarship repays the reader who perseveres.

Lawler, Donald L. "Oscar Wilde's First Manuscript of *The Picture of Dorian Gray*." *Studies in Bibliography* 25 (1972): 125–35. An important examination of the process of composition that informed Wilde's novel.

————. *An Inquiry into Oscar Wilde's Revisions of* The Picture of Dorian Gray. New York: Garland Publishing, 1988. Incorporating his earlier textual criticism of the novel, Lawler forms the most lucid and detailed examination now available of the various stages of Wilde's process of composition.

——, ed. *The Picture of Dorian Gray: Authoritative Texts, Backgrounds, Reviews and Reactions, Criticism*. New York: W. W. Norton, 1988. A scrupulously edited version of the novel, made even more useful by Lawler's decision to also include the 1890 *Lippincott's* version of *The Picture of Dorian Gray*. Also contains a fine collection of contemporaneous and contemporary reactions to Wilde's novel.

Lewis, Lloyd, and Henry Justin Smith. *Oscar Wilde Discovers America*. New York: Harcourt, 1936. A richly detailed account of Wilde's 1883 lecture tour of America. It remains a useful scholarly resource.

Manganiello, Dominic. "Ethics and Aesthetics in *The Picture of Dorian Gray*." *Canadian Journal of Irish Studies* 9 (December 1983): 25–33. Takes the position that "*The Picture of Dorian Gray* examines frankly the consequences of substituting an aesthetic for an ethical conscience." Although this thesis seems problematic, Manganiello does a good job outlining the issues at stake when examining how the novel deals with ethics and aesthetics.

Marcus, Steven. *The Other Victorians: A Study of Sexuality and Pornography in Mid-Nineteenth-Century England*. New York: Basic Books, 1966. The classic study of Victorian sexual attitudes. It provides useful insights into the sensuality that informed nineteenth-century English life.

Mason, Stuart [Christopher Millard]. *Bibliography of Oscar Wilde*. London: Laurie, 1914; rpt., London: Rota, 1967. A detailed and reliable overview of Wilde's canon and the early critical responses to his writings.

Mikhail, E. H. *Oscar Wilde: An Annotated Bibliography of Criticism*. London: Macmillan, 1978.

Moers, Ellen. *The Dandy: Brummell to Beerbohm*. Lincoln: University of Nebraska Press, 1960. A useful background study of a Victorian type whose behavior informs the roles assumed by many of the characters in *The Picture of Dorian Gray*.

Murray, Isobel. "Some Elements in the Composition of *The Picture of Dorian Gray*." *Durham University Journal* 64 (January 1972): 220–31. A scholarly examination of the editorial and compositional changes that occurred between the 1890 *Lippincott's* version of *The Picture of Dorian Gray* and the 1891 novel version. Murray's careful delineations of the differences in the two works sharpen one's sense of the artistic, aesthetic, and social values that shaped Wilde's writing.

Nassaar, Christopher. *Into the Demon Universe*. New Haven, Conn.: Yale University Press, 1974. A detailed study of Wilde's canon. Unfortunately, its interpretations fall victim to a humorless and circumscribing literalism antipathetic to Wilde's own approach to literature.

Paglia, Camille A. "Oscar Wilde and the English Epicene." *Raritan* 4, no. 3 (Winter 1985): 85–109. Paglia raises a number of important issues relating to how one reads Wilde's canon. The most interesting lies in her link between epicene humor and gender-oriented language. Unfortunately, Paglia's argument rests on generalizations that do not enjoy the advantage of logic or evidence to support them.

Powell, Kerry. *Oscar Wilde and the Theatre of the 1890s*. Cambridge: Cambridge University Press, 1990. Although this book does not deal directly with *The Picture of Dorian Gray*, it offers a wonderful overview of the cultural context in which Wilde wrote his most successful works.

———. "Tom, Dick, and Dorian Gray: Magic-Picture Mania in Late Victorian Fiction." *Philological Quarterly* 62 (Spring 1983): 147–70. A very thoughtful piece of analogical criticism that goes beyond the usual scope of influence studies to trace the impact of Gothic novels on the structure of *The Picture of Dorian Gray*.

Ransome, Arthur. *Oscar Wilde: A Critical Study*. London: Martin Secker, 1912; New York: Mitchell Kennerley, 1912. Considered by Ian Fletcher and John Stokes "the first genuinely critical book" on Wilde.

Roditi, Edouard. *Oscar Wilde*. Norfolk, Conn.: New Directions, 1947. A thematic reading of selected works that places Wilde in the tradition of the Dandy.

San Juan, Jr., Epifanio. *The Art of Oscar Wilde*. Princeton, N.J.: Princeton University Press, 1967. One of the earliest scholarly studies that both considered Wilde's entire canon and incorporated modern interpretive approaches into its format.

Sherard, Robert. *Oscar Wilde: The Story of an Unhappy Friendship*. London: privately printed, 1902; London: Greening, 1905.

Shewan, Rodney. *Oscar Wilde: Art and Egotism*. New York: Barnes & Noble, 1977. Considers Wilde's canon by blending a biographical approach with some textual criticism. In viewing Wilde as a lifelong romantic, Shewan reiterates views that had were long been critical commonplaces.

Small, Ian. "Semiotics and Oscar Wilde's Accounts of Art." *British Journal of Aesthetics* 25 (Winter 1985): 50–56. An attempt to offer a detailed account of Wilde's concept of art. As the title indicates, Small's study is a semiotic analysis of the significance of Wilde's remark that "Nature imitates Art." He makes a number of clear linguistic points but in doing so manages to drain all wit and freshness from Wilde's observation.

———. *Oscar Wilde Revalued: An Essay on New Materials and Methods of Research*. Greensboro, N.C.: ELT Press, 1993. A highly detailed survey of primary and secondary material relating to Wilde studies. Small provides an extremely lucid overview of Wilde criticism over the last 100 years and an extremely valuable account of the status and location of

Wilde manuscripts and other resources. An important research tool for anyone undertaking an in-depth examination of Wilde's canon.

Smith II, Philip E., and Michael S. Helfand, eds. *Oscar Wilde's Oxford Notebooks: A Portrait of Mind in the Making.* Oxford: Oxford University Press, 1989. Transcriptions of a notebook and a commonplace book kept by Wilde while he was at Oxford. This collection offers useful insights into the forces shaping Wilde's process of composition.

Spivey, Ted R. "Damnation and Salvation in *The Picture of Dorian Gray.*" *Boston University Studies in English* 4 (1960): 162–70. A view of Wilde's novel as an urbane version of a morality play.

Symons, Arthur. *A Study of Oscar Wilde.* London: Charles J. Sawyer, 1930; Folcroft, Penn.: Folcroft Press, 1969. A critical work from one of Wilde's contemporaries that takes a highly ambivalent position, by and large evincing a great deal more sympathy for Wilde's critical essays than for his creative writings.

Winwar, Frances. *Oscar Wilde and the Yellow Nineties.* New York: Harper and Bros., 1940. A study that approaches Wilde's life in terms of the shaping forces of the period. It anticipated by over 30 years the cultural criticism of the 1970s and the 1980s and lays down interpretive guidelines still useful to readers following such an approach.

Index

Index

Ruskin, John, 7, 10–11, 36, 113
St. James's Gazette, 22
Salvation Army, 4
San Juan, Epifanio, Jr., 26
Sartre, Jean-Paul, 19
Scholastics, 57
Scots Observer, 23
Second Boer War, 4
Sedgwick, Eve Kosofsky, 27
Shakespeare, William, 33–35, 98; *King Lear*, 72
Shaw, George Bernard, 4; *Major Barbara*, 4
Sherard, Robert, 24–25
Singleton, Adrian (character), 51
Small, Ian, 27
Snow White, 47, 77
Socrates, 55–56
Social Class, 3–5, 6–7, 15, 74–75
"Speranza." *See* Wilde, Jane Francesca Elgee
Stoics, 57
Stoddart, J. Marshall, 21
Stokes, John, 25

Trinity College, Dublin, 5

Vane, James (character) 15, 19, 75, 90
Vane, Sibyl (character) 15, 40, 44, 48–51, 64–67, 71, 75, 79, 84–87, 88
Victorian Age, 3–5, 7–10, 11, 15–16, 25–26, 62–63, 66–68, 70, 76–78, 80–81, 93, 98–99

Ward, William, 7
Ward, Lock and Company, 21–22
Wharton, Anne H., 23
Whistler, James A. McNeill, 10
Wilde, Isola, 5
Wilde, Jane Francesca Elgee, 6
Wilde, Oscar Fingal O'Flahertie Wills: birth of, 3; childhood in Ireland of, 5–6; death of, 12; early life in London of, 8–10; education of, 6–7; 1895 trial of, 9, 11, 59; imprisonment of, 11–12, 59

WORKS
"Ballad of Reading Gaol, The," 11
"Critic as Artist, The," 104
De Profundis, 11
Ideal Husband, An, 11
Importance of Being Earnest, The, 11, 27
"Lady Lancing," 27
"Magdalen Walks," 7
"Picture of Dorian Gray, The," (novella), 9, 21–23, 78, 92–93
Picture of Dorian Gray, The (novel): archetypes, 15, 26–27, 38, 118; beauty, 16–17, 38–39, 42–43, 45–48, 49–50, 76–77, 82, 86, 95; biographical associations, 9–11 24–26, 80–82, 110; characters, 9, 31–32, 43, 45, 75; composition, 3, 7, 9–11, 37, 93; grammar, 35–37; Hallward's painting, 16, 35–37, 38–42, 43, 45, 49–53, 71–72, 83, 89, 95; imagination, 39–41, 83–85, 87, 101, 104–6; language, 14–15, 27, 34–35; points of view, 13–14, 17–19, 32, 37–38, 40, 43–47, 49, 51–52, 72, 75, 92–106; revisions, 23–28, 93, 119–21; sexuality, 15, 27, 48–49, 51, 64, 76–87, 90–91; social context, 11, 15–16, 18, 24–26, 32, 55, 66, 75–78, 80–82, 93, 97, 118–19, 123; structure, 12, 13–15, 19, 31–32, 37, 39–41, 93, 100, 102–3; voyeurism, 46–47, 63–65

The Author

Michael Patrick Gillespie is Professor of English at Marquette University. He has written *Inverted Volumes Improperly Arranged: James Joyce and His Trieste Library* (1983), *A Catalogue of James Joyce's Trieste Library* (1986), *Reading the Book of Himself: Narrative Strategies in the Works of James Joyce* (1989), *Oscar Wilde: Life, Work, and Criticism* (1990), and *Joycean Occasions* (edited with Melvin Friedman and Janet Dunleavy, 1991). He has also published articles on a range of Irish and British writers.

ISBN-13: 978-0-8057-8375-9
ISBN-10: 0-8057-8375-X